FLECKS
OF GOLD
ON A PATH
OF STONE

Simple Truths for
Profound Living

CRAIG D. LOUNSBROUGH

AMBASSADOR INTERNATIONAL
GREENVILLE, SOUTH CAROLINA & BELFAST, NORTHERN IRELAND

www.ambassador-international.com

Flecks of Gold on a Path of Stone
Simple Truths for Profound Living

Printed in the United States of America

ISBN: 978-1-62020-116-9
eISBN: 978-1-62020-167-1

Cover design and typesetting: Matthew Mulder
E-book conversion: Anna Riebe

Cover Design: and Typesetting: Matthew Mulder
E-book conversion: Anna Riebe

AMBASSADOR INTERNATIONAL
Emerald House
427 Wade Hampton Blvd.
Greenville, SC 29609, USA
www.ambassador-international.com

AMBASSADOR BOOKS
The Mount
2 Woodstock Link
Belfast, BT6 8DD, Northern Ireland, UK
www.ambassador-international.com

The colophon is a trademark of Ambassador

Flecks of Gold
on a Path of Stone

Simple Truths for Profound Living

Craig D. Lounsbrough
M.Div, LPC

Contents

Preface 11

Introduction 13

SECTION ONE

Simple Truths for Profound Times

CHAPTER 1
Being Thankful: A Forgotten Art 19

CHAPTER 2
Christmas: A Sorely Needed Reclamation 25

CHAPTER 3
Seasons: The Come and Go of Life 31

CHAPTER 4
Spring Cleaning: Never Even Looking at the House 37

CHAPTER 5
The New Year: Clean Slate or Simply Stale? 43

CHAPTER 6
The Untimely: When It All Happens When It Shouldn't 49

CHAPTER 7
Sparrows in the Garage: Little Treasures 55

CHAPTER 8
Our Metronome: Timing 61

SECTION TWO

Simple Truths for Profound Relationships

CHAPTER 9
Fight or Flee: Our Contradictory Nature in Crisis. 69

CHAPTER 10
Loneliness: Agendas that Starve Relationships 75

CHAPTER 11
Loneliness: Communication that Starves Relationships. 81

CHAPTER 12
Loving Your Enemies: More Than a Nice Idea. 87

CHAPTER 13
Loving Your Enemies: Seeing Ourselves in Our Responses. 93

CHAPTER 14
Relationships: Double-Edged 99

SECTION THREE

Simple Truths for Profound Growth

CHAPTER 15
Our Identity and Value: Internal, Not External 107

CHAPTER 16
Releasing Your Grip: Possessing Life Is Letting Life Possess You. . . . 113

CHAPTER 17
Success: Defining It Defines Us 119

CHAPTER 18
Taking Ourselves Too Seriously: The Weight that We Carry 125

CHAPTER 19
The Bottom Line: What Drives Our Decisions 131

CHAPTER 20
The Worst Slavery: Slavery to Ignorance. 137

CHAPTER 21
Uniqueness: Looking Beyond Labels to See Strengths 143

CHAPTER 22
Uniqueness: Uniqueness Not as License 149

CHAPTER 23
What We Worship: The Things We Bow Down To 155

SECTION FOUR
Simple Truths for Profound Wisdom

CHAPTER 24
Common Sense: Having Lost All Sense 163

CHAPTER 25
Consequences: Trying to Sidestep the Inevitable 169

CHAPTER 26
Experience: Living, Saving, or Forgetting 175

CHAPTER 27
Fill 'er Up: It's Never Lasting 181

CHAPTER 28
Have We Forgotten?: Lulled to Sleep 187

CHAPTER 29
Historical Revisionist: Our Fear of Truth 193

CHAPTER 30
Miraculous to the Mundane:
Refusing to Lose the Wonder and Privilege 199

CHAPTER 31
Pain to Paralysis: Coming Apart at the Scars 205

CHAPTER 32
Playing with Fire: Thinking We're That Good 211

CHAPTER 33
Reality: The Extent of Your Reach 217

SECTION FIVE

Simple Truths for Profound Living

CHAPTER 34
Carrying It All: Ownership Versus "On Loan" 225

CHAPTER 35
Dad's Workbench: There's a Tool for That 231

CHAPTER 36
Killing the Sacred: Bludgeoning the Heart Out of Life 237

CHAPTER 37
Left Lane Living: Driving at the Speed of Life 243

CHAPTER 38
Lemmings and Sheep: The Role of Boundaries and Rules 249

CHAPTER 39
Magnificent Living: Taking Things for Granted 255

CHAPTER 40
Mining Memories: The Tool of Memories 261

CHAPTER 41
Traditions: A Sorely Needed Grounding 267

CHAPTER 42
"Now I Lay Me Down to Sleep": Mom and Dad's Bedtime Prayer 273

Conclusion 279

Preface

IT'S BRILLIANTLY MYSTERIOUS HOW A series of random thoughts merge to coalesce into other thoughts. Those thoughts can be entirely unexpected, thoroughly tantalizing, and wildly vibrant. Those intermingling and intertwining thoughts never would have happened had they not been prefaced by the thoughts that came before them. Out of this very intentional randomness, wonderful things are born that otherwise may never have been born. This book is a result of such a mysterious alchemy.

If I were to backtrack along the chain of events that led to the book you hold in your hands, the path would wind back to my childhood. Standing firm and ever consistent were my parents. They were born of hardy stock, reared in the black grip of the great Depression, called to face the dark threats of the Second World War, and raised to raise a nation once the war ended and the challenges of building a nation began. They were people of rooted ethics, clear morals, and immovable values. For them, there was never a question of compromise.

It's from their example that I saw how to live out the core truths in a world of accelerating complexities. They were always able to reach back to a simpler, destitute time and draw from it an endless array of simple truths that made our lives everything they could possibly be. From their example, I learned that profound complexities could always be intersected, dismantled, and resolved with little more than a handful of profoundly simple truths. I watched them do it magnificently. And so, as with the first book, I commit this text to Mom and Dad. I am immeasurably blessed by both of you.

An early writing mentor once told me that, next to heavy lifting, writing was the most difficult thing that he had ever done. I could only concur with the wisdom and reality of that statement through my own writing experiences. In my writing career, I have sprinted full force and sometimes strolled into walls and barriers that laid me prostrate. I have slogged through the muck of frustration and been pressed to my knees by the angst of writer's block and literary self-doubt. There were very real moments when I questioned my ability to effectively put pen to paper and do what I'd set out to do.

In those times, the thoughts of my two children gave me a sustaining strength and driving motivation that propelled me onward despite the walls and muck. It was seeing the vast potential in each of them that allowed me to see how good two young people can be and how much hope there is for the future. That epiphany stirred my desire to try to bring a ray of light to the future that they are walking into so that the future of their generation might be a bit brighter. And so, as with the first book, I likewise commit this book to Cheyenne and Corey. You are both an inspiration in ways you can't understand. I love you both deeply, I pray for you both daily, and I thank God that I am somehow worthy to be called your Dad.

Finally, I extend a profound thanks to all those at Ambassador International who faithfully and rigorously partnered with me in the creation of this book. I cherish your commitment to God, your passion for the craft of publishing, and your always-fresh vision. It has been a privileged journey.

Introduction

I HAVE SPENT YEARS IN pursuit of the treasures of knowledge, wisdom, and discernment. I have plunged into the depths of what sometimes seems to be the endless study of endless subjects. I have plumbed the deep caverns of knowledge. I have set myself to be immersed in experiences of the widest array that time and resources would permit. As the years have rolled on, I have accelerated that endeavor with an ever-increasing commitment and speed. It has been a great journey indeed.

Despite how much one may know, there is always more to learn. As part of that journey, one thing I have learned: simple truths are simply powerful. Simple truths seem grossly inadequate in our complex world. They don't seem to speak too much of anything vital, nor do they appear to have any power to effectively engage, manage, or much less offset the dizzying complexities in our world. The simple truths seem archaic and rusty, being relics of simpler times with the weeds of irrelevancy having grown up around them. The simple truths are fun to toy with as some sort of intellectual amusement or philosophical play, but their relevancy lies in their irrelevancy. Our sense is that our world has long out-paced them, rendering them genuinely nice ideas that are insufficient in dealing with the realities of this complex world of ours.

It's indeed odd that we so readily discard the "old" in favor of the new. We forget that "old" in age typically does not mean "old" in terms of relevance. To immediately connect "old" with "irrelevant" robs life of some of its most precious treasures and irreplaceable truths. In fact, the most powerful, fundamental and meaningful things in our lives are old in terms of time but perpetually new and ever fresh in terms of relevance. Yet, we carelessly equate old with irrelevant and throw it out based on our sense that it just isn't applicable anymore. We throw away treasure and in most cases replace it with trash.

We do the same with simple truths. Yet, complexities are in reality born of simple truths. Every complexity can be decisively engaged with the simple truths that undergird it and hold it together. However large, daunting, difficult, tangled, or complicated a situation or circumstance might be, at its foundation there are simple truths that birthed it and continue to sustain it. We just don't see them anymore. It's in the thorough reclamation and wise application of these simple truths that we can overcome. Articulating those truths in both a succinct and yet expansive manner, then competently tying them to life's complexities, renders those truths as tremendously valuable and strikingly relevant, regardless of the complexities that we face.

The simple truths remove massive obstacles and provide stunning clarity to life's challenges. The simple truths inspire us and ground us in truths and realities that are core to who we are, embedding us in facts and principles that are unchangeable and unshakeable. Simple truths dispel confusion, provide direction, and make sense of that which seems utterly and irrevocably senseless.

This book is about simple truths richly explained, practically expanded upon, and relevantly integrated into life's realities in a manner that brings fresh insight and desperately needed resources to all of us who struggle. It's about getting back to the basics in order to master the complexities. It's about getting grounded to be granted successes. Simply . . . it's about embracing the reality that simple truths are simply powerful.

This book represents a journey of helping people that encompasses a span of ten years in pastoral ministry and twenty-three years in the counseling field. It's in that tumultuous and terribly rewarding journey that I found that grappling with the complexities in tens of thousands of lives also meant unearthing the simple truths that undergirded those complexities. Sometimes that meant that the complexities could be removed altogether, rapidly moving the person toward liberation and health. At other times, it left the complexities intact, instead providing powerful tools to engage the complexities, disarm them, dismantle them, destroy them, and move the person forward in a manner freed and restored. Either way, simple truths forged a path to profound healing and wholeness.

This book is a partial collection of those truths as I have bumped into them or stumbled over them in my work with people. It's also part of my own journey as my life has more than once been laid scorched and barren. Whether in my life or the lives of others, these truths have been remarkably restorative and reinvigorating. They have exhibited a power that I could not have imagined, a power that I have come to cherish. It's my deepest hope that within these pages you are likewise restored and reinvigorated. Indeed, may you be transformed not by this book but by the timeless truths cited within its pages. May they speak to some point in your journey or to the whole of your journey. Here's wishing you the power of simple truths to transform your life.

SECTION ONE

Simple Truths for Profound Times

CHAPTER 1

Being Thankful:
A Forgotten Art

*"With them were Heman and Jeduthun and the rest of those chosen
and designated by name to* **give thanks to the LORD,** *"for his love
endures forever"* *[emphasis mine].*

—1 Chronicles 16:14

"Thanksgiving comes to us out of the prehistoric dimness,
Universal to all ages and all faiths.
At whatever straws we must grasp,
There is always a time for gratitude and new beginnings."

—J. Robert Moskin

BEING THANKFUL IS A GENUINELY nice idea. It's an
action that we feel obligated to take, one of those socially appropriate courtesies that we're supposed to adhere to because it's just the
right thing to do. There's something respectable, proper, good, fitting,
and simply wholesome about being thankful. It rounds us up and
rounds us out. A feeling of thankfulness orients us by grounding
us in a stabilizing sense of appreciation that doesn't allow things to
become too important or too unimportant. Thankfulness allows us

to walk through a world inundated by opportunities and possessions, being slaves to neither nor, at the other extreme, finding ourselves cavalier and careless in our handling of them.

The Reasons Not to Be Thankful

However, lodged somewhere in the background of our minds, we often see thankfulness as kind of tritely nostalgic. It seems more like a pleasant social courtesy from a time long past that doesn't have any leverage to get us where we want to go today. It's all about the refined social courtesies and languishing behaviors of some bygone Elizabethan era populated by top hats and poufy dresses. Being thankful sometimes seems outmoded and outdated. It really doesn't get us much of anything anyway, so why do it?

Then there's the haste of life where we don't feel that we have time to be thankful. Or if we do have time to ponder or pontificate about our lives, we often feel that our situation isn't really the kind of situation that we should be all that thankful about. Sometimes life is more about survival and less about anything else. Life is often about the rigors of simply staying afloat in the choppy whitecaps of life's turbulent seas. We can't get a break. Instead, we're always being broken. Life isn't cutting us any slack; rather, it's cutting us to pieces. Our sweetest dreams have curdled into sour discouragement. So there doesn't seem to be any rationale for being thankful because there's nothing really abounding or overflowing or anything that we'd honestly be able to describe or define as a blessing. Tecumseh, the Shawnee Chief, said, "If you see no reason for giving thanks, the fault lies with yourself." So does the fault lie with us, or does it lie with a stingy, miserly world that penny-pinches us to death?

Our Criteria of Thankfulness

Being thankful is an action that we reserve for the special stuff, the stuff that's above and beyond. We're thankful when something really great happens, or when we have a fortunate turn of events, or when things fall our way, or when we get what we perceive as a long overdue break. We're thankful when life really steps up in our favor and grants us a reprieve or cuts us some slack. There's a sense that we need to express some sort of thanks when things break in our direction, there's a spree of good fortune, or life smiles on us and rains down a blessing or two or three or more. It's when there's a flurry of good stuff, or some load lightens, or we get a well-deserved break. That's when we're supposed to be thankful. Give us a reason to be thankful and we'll probably be thankful. If what comes our way doesn't smack of something outstanding, we see it as just a bunch of hullabaloo and hot air. If it doesn't pass muster, we're just going to allow it to pass on. Hand us an event or circumstance or turn of events that's truly great and we'll be grateful. Otherwise, what's the sense?

CHEAP THANKFULNESS

We assume that a sense of thanks or thankfulness is based on the receipt of some gift or privilege or promising opportunity. Thankfulness is a cordial "tipping of the hat" to some courtesy that life or some person has afforded us. We feel that being thankful is a response tenaciously reserved for those times when something is being granted or given to us. It's the natural outcome and right response of having things go our way, getting a break of some sort, or simply having life lavish some good fortune upon us. Thankfulness is contingent upon our receiving some gracious favor for which we express a sense of gratefulness and gratitude.

But that makes thankfulness something cheap and shallow. If giving something back because we got something in the first place is what thankfulness is really all about, then it only exists when it's all good, or we're on the receiving end of some blessing or favorable turn of events. It has absolutely no inherent value of its own, and it's only granted value as some act of socially appropriate courtesy. Is thankfulness really that cheap, that thin, and that superficial? Have we gutted it to the point that it's just a medium of exchange and nothing more? Is its value only as some token that we trade for some success or bit of good fortune? Is it little more than a social formality that's due only if a decision or course of action works out for us?

What's Our Attitude?

Our view of thankfulness reflects our attitude. We've lost an appreciation for life, and our attitude reflects that. We see life as something we have to chase after, accumulate, and often hoard. In the chasing, accumulating, and hoarding, it becomes all about what we don't have. What we don't have then drives what we want to have. We inventory our lives, we make a tedious tally of the innumerable things we don't have but think we should have, and then we generate some sort of golden shopping list that drives everything else that we do. We're on a mad hunt for the successes or possessions that we feel we want or are entitled to have. And when these things are achieved or obtained, we're thankful. When they aren't, we're not.

What's Our Perspective?

An anonymous author wrote that "some people are always grumbling because roses have thorns; I am thankful that thorns have roses." That's perspective. What's our perspective? Are our minds so rigidly landlocked that our entire focus is on what we don't have, or what's not comfortable, or what's contrary to our goals, or how far we haven't come? What is it that we see, anyway? Is disappointment all we see, what hasn't worked, the stuff we haven't been able to check off our lists, the rungs that we haven't been able to ascend on whatever ladder we've put ourselves on, the pinnacles that others have ascended that we haven't? Is that all we see? If that's all, then there's absolutely no room and certainly no rationale for thankfulness. In fact, there may indeed be no tolerance for it.

Thankfulness is about an appreciation regardless of where we're at or what hits us. It recognizes life as a privilege, despite how difficult living out this privilege can be. It's an inherent belief that life is sacred and, ultimately, that life is good. Thankfulness recognizes that we have the immense privilege of struggle and the far-reaching opportunity of failure because we likewise have the ability to mine deep, transforming lessons out of both. It's being thankful that the thorns in our lives, despite how many there might be, always have roses somewhere if we look for them. So what are we going to focus on, the thorns or the roses?

Thankfulness rests not on what we have, but on what's possible. Not on what we possess, but on what's ours to enjoy without the burden of possession. Thankfulness is a deep appreciation for the lavish gifts of life that sometimes come packaged in the gift wrap of pain and loss. Thankfulness is realizing that the pleasure of the small things radically outweighs possession of the big things. Real thankfulness rests in the reality of ceaseless opportunity, the endless ability to savor a bit of good fortune or a benevolent act as new and fresh. Authentic thankfulness acknowledges the existence of limitless challenges and the ever-abounding transitions of life that offer us innumerable new paths to explore.

Yes, sometimes this stuff doesn't appear to have any shred of good in it at all. Sometimes it looks all bad only because we haven't developed the vision to see the good that looms rich and full behind the bad. Sometimes all we see are endlessly tangled vines with savage thorns and not a rose in sight. We don't see roses, because we're not looking for them. But because we're not looking for them doesn't in any way mean that they're not there; we've just chosen not to see them. And if we don't see them, we won't be thankful for them.

An Attitude of Thanks

In the New Testament, Paul said that we are to give thanks always for everything. That's a tall order. We're to give thanks for everything because in everything there is always something to be thankful for—if we can just get past the anger, disappointment, and frustration in order to see it. It's an exercise of faith—faith in the fact that life is a whole lot bigger than we perceive it to be. It's about a faith that life grants ever-increasing opportunities that run right alongside of and outrun the losses we're experiencing. It's realizing that life is not about possession, but realizing that while we can't possess everything, we can enjoy everything without the onerous burden of possession. Finally, it's just realizing that despite it all, life is a privilege, despite the fact that it might not feel that way at times. Because all of these are authentically underlying foundational realities of life, there will always be room to be thankful. Maybe we need to rethink our attitudes, push aside the thorns, and reach for the roses.

CHAPTER 2

Christmas: A Sorely Needed Reclamation

"The people walking in darkness have seen a great light; on those living in the land of deep darkness a light has dawned."
—Isaiah 9:2

"It came without ribbons! It came without tags! It came without packages, boxes or bags!" Then the Grinch thought of something he hadn't before! "Maybe Christmas," he thought, "doesn't come from a store. Maybe Christmas...perhaps...means a little bit more!"
—Dr. Seuss, *How the Grinch Stole Christmas!*

SOME THIRTY YEARS AGO, I was given the opportunity to be a part of the reclamation of a gorgeous, seventy-three room colonial-style mansion, as well as the property and numerous out-buildings that were part of this massive, rolling estate. It had set empty, hauntingly still, and seemingly comatose for several decades with suffocating layers of dust, endless rooms marred to embarrassment by peeling paint, and massive walls stripped nearly naked by faded and peeling wallpaper. All of the morbid decay was edged by generations of lacey cobwebs that seemed like thin, sporadically hung sheets of tissue paper. There was something terribly sad and forlorn about it all, like when something majestic is abandoned and entirely forgotten in the abandonment, like beauty relegated to oblivion.

It was all a very odd and strange sort of dichotomy in that one could clearly see the tremendous architectural beauty of the buildings, the opulent and exquisite designs within and without, as well as the ornate landscaping hidden behind the scrub of decay and inattention. It was a jewel far too grand to be so easily lost in the miry and mischievous hands of rot. If you looked closely, and if you squinted the eyes of your soul sufficiently, you could make out scant traces of a glorious kind of majesty huddling quietly under the pathetic morass of deterioration.

Dilapidated, seemingly sullen, and plummeting into pathetic disrepair, the endlessly rich and prolific artistry of the architecture, as well as the meticulous attention to detail that had gone into landscaping the massive grounds, was all still there—if you had eyes patient enough to see it. Our eyes are more than willing to see the good stuff, the easy stuff, and the fun stuff, the stuff we want to cheer about, croon over, and celebrate. We're all about that. But what about seeing the horrific travesty of grandeur that has become something gutted and grotesque? What about seeing majesty that's now mangled? What about seeing a hint of horribly tarnished glory that held a scant but absolutely captivating reflection of what life was supposed to be like—that was killed by what life actually turned out to be like? That kind of stuff we have to be willing to see because it involves facing how far we are from how far we could have been.

It was obvious that the whole estate was a wonderfully marvelous creation that had been utterly lost, that a treasure had been carelessly handed off to disregard, and that glory had been ground underfoot by gross disregard for the glory. Yet, it was something that was not so lost that it couldn't be reclaimed and restored to its former glory.

The results of abandonment and foolish disregard could be undone if one had eyes willing to see beyond the carnage of decay, a heart bent on reclaiming that which should never have been lost, and an unshakeable belief in what once was, which drove the belief that "what was" could be once again.

CHRISTMAS LOST

Christmas seems achingly hollow, as if the warmly beating heart of the holiday has been disregarded. It seems that it might have been a time rich, wonderful, and life-transforming. It has become like the old, abandoned estate. Christmas has been marred to embarrassment and stripped naked. It seems more like a tossed relic, being an ever so slight handful of leftover pieces and parts of a bejeweled gift that at one time was precious beyond description. There's something inherently majestic in this holiday that has been abandoned by us, something flippantly cast aside, something that was foolishly abandoned and tragically forgotten in the abandonment. And so it has set, for who knows how long, in decay and disrepair.

In many ways, Christmas seems like a limp rag that's been rung nearly dry. We have some tiny bit of essence of it left, some scent of golden essence, some priceless nard that still has a very slight aroma and a scant bit of remaining dampness. But we've pretty much rung the very life out of it. It has all of the timeless substance that makes something splendidly grand; something that's infinitely more substantial than repetitive carols, gaudy rolls of wrapping paper, tangled strands of twinkling lights, cutesy cards, as well as festivities of sordid sorts that all seem something of a slight shadow, a nearly indistinct footprint, a nearly lost scent of something that once was, but now is not.

And now we're left with what too often seems like empty tradition, repetitive rituals, and substance-less substance that wear us out to the point that we have no remaining energy to celebrate it once we've got it all set up to celebrate. We've stripped and discarded a season that is so little of what it once was—or maybe should have been—that we tend to celebrate more vigorously when the season humanely rolls off the calendar and is over than we did while it was actually going on.

STRIPPED AND BARREN

Why do we do what we do with life? What is Christmas, anyway? Where did this all come from? Why have we flippantly discarded the core of it and gutted it to the point that it's less the resilient pulse of vibrant life and more the sluggish beat of rote and ritual? Maybe we should ask why it hasn't really worked that well since we gutted it. Maybe we ought to consider that our tendency to improve on everything only diminishes great things.

Do we also gut the very life out of other areas of our existence? We seem to take license to make things what we want them to be. And what we want them to be are thoughtlessly rote actions that don't demand anything of us, that don't have any annoying rules that hem us in, and that don't come affixed with ethics or morals that might cause us to feel any twinge of guilt. We want permission to be permissive, so we gut things to make them permissive. Yet, when we do that, we remove the heart of them. We do that with life and with Christmas.

WHAT IS CHRISTMAS?

That question will be answered differently by different people according to their belief systems, backgrounds, personal experiences, and biases. There's not sufficient time or space here to engage that question fully. However, I think that we know a few things:

Christmas is a whole lot more than we've allowed it to be, or caused it to be, whichever the case might be. There's a spirit of sorts that's inherently deep in this season that's somehow core to each of us. Christmas bespeaks a desire to believe that hope is worth hoping in, that the world has the potential to be better than it's become, and that each one of us is something more than we've allowed ourselves to believe. Christmas seems to say that paradise lost and longed for does not have to be paradise given up on. That all the good that we hope for is indeed reasonable to hope for, and that there's real power and potential to make that "good" more of a reality than a dream.

I think we know that Christmas somehow exposes the hidden richness of all humanity. It gives reason and opportunity for humanity to prove its worth by turning on itself with grace, being merciful to others, loving lavishly (which includes loving oneself), and stepping up on behalf of our fellow man rather than stepping away from him. Christmas is about knowing that whatever we're all worth, it's enough to be sacrificed for, which means we're worth a whole lot. It's a vision that illustrates in broad relief an indispensable part of life that's been lost while delivering a timeless and passionate plea to restore what's been lost. It's a belief that what's been lost should have never been lost in the first place. It's a conviction that all of this can yet be redeemed and that a provision of perfect proportions has been made for that to happen. It's a message of worth and hope—total worth and endless hope. It's the kind of message that's infinitely bigger than all of us but is offered to all of us.

In time, the old mansion and grounds of the estate were restored to their original splendor. Because of that, there's been a reversal of sorts. The photos from thirty years ago tell the story of the peeling paint, faded wallpaper, overgrown grounds, and the dilapidated state of it all. They are photos of what was once lost, what it all once looked like. Yet, there were those who refused to let be it be lost, and they reclaimed it. It is now wondrous indeed, possibly better than it ever was. Christmas is lost in disrepair, but it remains to be wholly and marvelously reclaimed.

CHAPTER 3

Seasons: The Come and Go of Life

"He changes times and seasons; he deposes kings and raises up others. He gives wisdom to the wise and knowledge to the discerning."
—Daniel 2:21

"To be interested in the changing seasons is a happier state of mind than to be hopelessly in love with spring."
—George Santayana

SEASONS AND LOSS . . . each are part and parcel of the other. Life is fluid. It's always changing in ways that we may sometimes see but more often don't—or at least don't entirely recognize. We can't halt change, either as a means of holding on to something we don't want to lose or to avoid something that we fear is going to happen. We can't put the brakes on change to keep us from being ever distanced from some sort of cherished past. There is no moment when all stands completely still so that we can catch our breath. We don't have the convenience of starting, stopping, or somehow modulating change. The bills will come. The wrinkles will form. Snow will fly. Flowers will grow, and metal will rust. Days will peel off calendars faster than we can imagine, and years will fall off our lives like leaves falling off trees on a blustery autumn day. For better or for worse, we're on a ride that knows nothing of stops and exists only to progress. That's how life works.

CHANGE MEANS LOSS AS MUCH AS GAIN

Yet in many ways, we abhor change because a large part of change involves the reality of loss. Change is loss and loss is change. We cannot change without experiencing loss. If loss were not a part of the equation, we would soon become so terribly encumbered by the mass amassing of our experiences and assorted acquisitions that life would eventually kill us all. Loss provides balance. It maintains a sleekness. It keeps us clean. It cuts the fat, trims the waste, jettisons the collective baggage of our hording tendencies, and refuses to let slothfulness find leg room at the table of our lives. To do that, it's constantly going to peel away the fears, apprehensions, and misgivings that may impede our future.

If we are to change and if we are to move forward and progress, loss is an unalterable part of it all. In fact, the oddity of it may be that the most powerful, stimulating, and growth-inducing part of change is the loss that we experience in change. More times than not, loss is the indisputable yet seemingly unconventional key to gain. Loss frees us up and grows us up. Loss grants us priceless perspective, desperately needed mobility, ever-refreshing clarity, and a freeing tidiness. Loss decisively removes stubborn roadblocks, and it shakes us awake when we're lulled to sleep by the lullabies of complacency. Loss makes room for all the things that the future is delivering or about to deliver. So the very thing that we want to avoid is the very thing that may benefit us the most.

DEFINING LOSS ONLY AS LOSS

We typically define loss as simply that . . . loss. Loss comes in various ways. Sometimes it's a result of our own choices, whether those choices are those we've made intentionally or those we've made unintentionally. Either way, we caused it. Other times, loss is entirely out of our control, the result of someone else's choices or a series of circumstances that have come together through events or situations that we had no hand in creating and often didn't even know was happening. Sometimes loss is nothing more than a natural part of life, a normal progression of how it all works.

Sometimes loss is right and healthy. At other times, it's cruel and unfair. Sometimes we can recoup the loss or replace it with something greater than whatever it was that we lost. At other times, the hole remains empty, dark, and painful. Sometimes loss makes sense, but at other times, it makes no sense at all, despite how much we want to make sense of it. Loss can be viewed as timely, timeless, or entirely time-ignorant. What it does, it does. Yet, it naturally carries a negative stigma that we rarely question, and because we don't, we miss the opportunities and positive progression that could often be a natural outcome of our loss.

MISSED OPPORTUNITY BECAUSE OF A SKEWED VIEW

We don't conceptualize loss as part of the very natural ebb and flow of life, where things come and go in some sort of natural rhythm. We don't see loss as letting something (whose time has possibly come) go. We don't view it as a time, relationship, or opportunity that leaves so that something else new and potentially grander can take its place. We don't see it as being a time to close down one part of our lives in order to dramatically open up an entirely new and fresh part somewhere else. In loss, we can't see beyond the loss itself to the purpose inherent in the loss. And we typically can't do that for two fundamental reasons.

First, we automatically and quite naturally focus on the pain involved. Sometimes, to varying degrees, we can predict loss. However,

experiencing an actual loss is much, much different from the anticipation of it. In anticipating pain, we take it upon ourselves to assume
how the pain is going to feel or how it's all going to play itself out.
Most often the actual intensity of the pain, the timing of the pain,
the nature of the pain, and the reverberations of the pain are such
that it's in large part unanticipated and unexpected. We don't predict
it all that well. Therefore, it consumes the entirety of attention; in
other words, we become engulfed in it because it wasn't exactly what
we anticipated or planned for. The pain that we feel in loss is most
often very significant because it's never quite what we expected. This
dynamic can make the pain in loss both deep and frightening—like
an emotional tornado that tosses us wherever it pleases.

Second, because of the intensity of the pain, our focus is on the
pain rather than the actual loss itself. Initially we feel the loss as well
as the pain associated with loss. However, at times the intensity of
the pain itself replaces the actual loss; in essence, pain becomes both
the source and cause of our loss as it displaces the loss itself. All
we're paying attention to is the pain. Oddly enough, the loss is lost.
We're focused largely on our pain rather than grieving the loss that
caused our pain in the first place. With the focus on the pain alone,
we obviously get no resolution to the loss.

EBB AND FLOW – COME AND GO

Many times, we're not attuned to what's transpiring in our lives.
We're not attentive to the larger picture—to a grander scheme that's
bigger than just preserving the status quo. We're typically focused
on preserving the gains we think we've obtained and solidifying the
aspects of our lives that we feel give us a sense of security. We lock
whole areas of our lives down in our efforts to construct what we
perceive to be a life that's safe, secure, and stable. Or we lock it down
to avoid what we think's coming so maybe we can stop it. Anything
that jeopardizes the status quo that we perceive as providing us stability is seen as the enemy and a creeping threat that we adamantly
stand against. Therefore, change is bad.

A Different View of Loss

While preserving those stable areas of our lives can be wise, this preservation must be tempered with the reality that, in many instances, change and loss can actually birth greater stability. Change often involves loss, which is seen as destabilizing. Yet, if we are daring enough to embrace the larger picture, loss is often the precursor to a host of things that import deeper stability and integrate a more profound security. Walt Disney said, "All the adversity I've had in my life, all my troubles and obstacles, have strengthened me. You may not realize it when it happens, but a kick in the teeth may be the best thing in the world for you." Loss then is not necessarily an event that robs, but an intentional occurrence that purposefully removes certain things in order to make room for better things.

The problem is that loss brings temporary instability by virtue of the loss itself. The stability that loss can ultimately bring is often a pending stability that's down the road a bit and a whole lot less immediate than we'd prefer. Wisdom involves making changes and embracing loss in the present with an eye toward the long-term outcome of enhanced stability in the future. Loss is an investment in the very things that we think loss is causing us to lose. Quite often, loss is the very avenue through which all the things we fear losing are actually obtained, deepened, solidified, and expanded. Such is both the marvel and oddity of loss.

Loss as Necessity

If we really want to maximize the life that we have, and if we are desirous of living fully and broadly, we must be willing to experience loss. Loss is the building block to something greater. Loss clears away that which is dead, expended, outdated, or completed. It makes room to build upon the relationships, finances, opportunities, or a million other things that we've lost, assuming that the things we've lost were part of a larger progression of growth in our lives. Loss is part of gain. It's a natural process where gain is the ultimate outcome and loss is a part of that process, not the final outcome of that process. Loss is journey, not destination; a step, not the point of stepping off. Loss is fundamental to gain, not the end-game.

Maybe we need to move beyond the pain attached to loss and the apprehension regarding the instability we think it creates. Maybe we need a bigger vision that embraces loss as a natural phenomenon that creates space for something new and enhanced to come into our lives. Maybe we need to be less concerned for security and more concerned about growth.

Maybe we need to be a whole lot less present-focused and whole lot more possibility-focused. We just might need to realize that security and stability are important but not paramount. Maybe we need to embrace loss not because of the pain that comes with it, but because of the possibilities inherent in it.

Rethink your loss. Underneath the pain, there's probably a whole lot more promise than you thought.

CHAPTER 4

Spring Cleaning: Never Even Looking at the House

"Tremble and do not sin; when you are on your beds, search your hearts and be silent."

—Psalm 4:4

"The trouble with living alone is that it's always your turn to do the dishes."

—Author Unknown

CLEANING: IT'S THE UPKEEP SIDE of life. It's the drudgery that always follows us around with broom in hand. Cleaning is the voracious vacuum that's never satisfied, the frantic feather duster that spreads more dust than it captures, and the less than palatable reality that things don't clean themselves. Cleaning is dirt management. The imagery is one of a collection of plastic buckets, dripping mops, obnoxiously scented cleaning supplies, deteriorating sponges of assorted colors, latex gloves, and sweat. Who has time to clean? Much less, who wants to clean?

The definition of cleaning in the Encarta Dictionary is "the activity of making things clean, usually in a domestic or commercial environment." It seems that even the definition of cleaning is redundant. Sadly, cleaning tends to carry a negative connotation to it. It's just one of those things that we tend to grimace about when we have to do it or even think about doing it. It's not on our top ten list of the most engaging things to do. There's an old African Proverb that says, "When making a fire, people like to join you; when cleaning the ashes, you are often alone." There are two sides to most of life: doing something, and cleaning up after we've done it. Most of us like the first part but not the second.

Cleaning seems oddly self-defeating as well. We clean things knowing full well that we're going to have to clean again. It's not like there's anything of real permanence to what we're doing. Cleaning is not an effort that we can complete and feel some sustaining pride in; we're going to have to do what we just did all over again, in just the same way we just did it. There is no conclusion to the process of cleaning. What's frustrating is that you can't eliminate dirt; you can only move it from place to place. Therefore, we never come to a point where it's done forever and ever.

If you think about it further, cleaning as an action is not about obtaining more of what we have or something in addition to what we have. It has nothing to do with the acquisition of anything, nor does it have anything to do with the improvement or advancement of some object, task, or goal. Cleaning adds nothing to our lives except cleanliness, and that's only temporary. In terms of resources, assets, or improvements, it gains us none at all.

Rather, cleaning is energy and time that we have to put into maintaining what we already have. Cleaning in and of itself is an acknowledgement that nothing's permanent and that everything requires maintenance. The acquisition of some item or goal doesn't insure the continuation of that thing. Cleaning clearly lets us know that. We can buy it, barter it, order it, build it, swap it, charge it, win it, and even steal it, but we're going to have to clean it. Such is the dusty and dirty reality of life.

OUR LIVES

Too often, our lives are all about the acquisition of things but not the maintenance of them. In reference to ourselves personally, we have been bred with a fierce mentality of acquisition, whether that's the acquisition of education, licenses, certificates, knowledge, expertise, wisdom, social acumen, spiritual depth, or whatever it might be. It might be about vigorously cultivating our gifts, talents, and natural abilities. Such goals are certainly healthy and admirable. But in the obtaining and cultivating, do we ever do any cleaning? Do we ever even come close to realizing that things just don't perpetuate themselves? Does it dawn on us that if we don't clean, what we've amassed can be diminished by the accumulation of filth?

RATIONALIZING NOT CLEANING

An unknown author wrote, "Law of Window Cleaning: It's on the other side." We don't do a whole lot of personal cleaning because we like to think, "it's on the other side." We're all about acquisition and growth, but not much about personal cleaning: going through the various rooms, crawl spaces, nooks and crannies of our lives, getting on our knees to do some serious spring cleaning regardless of what time of year it is. That's not our focus, because it's not our preference. Cleaning is a distant sidebar to a much larger agenda. It's really not all that imperative. Dust never killed anyone, and who knows? A little dirt might be good for the soul! A few cobwebs aren't going to rot anything, and a handful of dust bunnies aren't going to do anything other than roll around a little. Besides, if there's really all that much dirt, it's "on the other side" anyway. So why clean?

Seeing dirt "on the other side" is really about choosing to ignore the dirt in our lives. Cleaning is about dirt. If it weren't for dirt, we wouldn't clean. Dirt is as much a reality of our lives as are the things that we amass. We prefer to ignore the dirt—because it demands that we take action to clean it up, hide it, or relocate it. But more than that, we appear to ignore dirt because we want to believe that we're *above* dirt. We want to believe that dirt doesn't collect in our lives, that we've outgrown the whole dirt thing, and that dirt is the stuff everyone else deals with. *We're* clean. *We're* good people. *We're* ethical. We don't have any dirt, and if we do, it's just a scant bit of it at best.

When we make that assumption and live in that manner, we set ourselves up to dramatically let ourselves down. Exactly what kind of dirt are we talking about? What are our cobwebs really? And those dust bunnies, what are they?

Our Dirt

We all have dirt, and probably lots of it. Some of our dirt is shameful, and some of it is outright embarrassing. Maybe some of our dirt is immoral, unethical, and possibly illegal. Maybe our dirt is a choice that we made to short-sheet an employer, short-circuit a relationship, or short-change a friend. It's possible that our dirt is a layered collection of lies, distortions, and rationalizations that we rigorously fabricated in order to dump our dirt on someone else. Maybe our dirt has been carted along with us for years and years because we could never bring ourselves to deal with it. It's possible that our dirt is a betrayal or an abandonment of a person or a belief system. Maybe it's a blatant rejection or a wound that we intentionally inflicted.

It might be that our dirt is brand spanking new; therefore, we've either rushed in our panic to hide it, or we have no idea what to do with it—so we walk around in it. It might be that our dirt isn't even something that we've done yet, but something that we plan to do. Maybe our dirt isn't about an action at all. Maybe it's about an attitude, about hating someone, being jealous, wishing ill for someone, or harboring a spirit of resentment. Maybe it's our unwillingness to forgive, or let go, or let the past be the past. Our dirt can be a whole bunch of different things, but it's still dirt.

Accountability – Saying "Yes, I Have Dirt"

Who wants to admit that they're dirty? More than that, who wants to admit how dirty their dirt really is? The hard truth is that some of our dirt is pathetic and raunchy. We're covered in some pretty reeking and outright foul stuff. Denying it doesn't remove it, and in no way does denial sweeten it. Placing blame and rationalizing and justifying won't change the reality of our dirt any more than cleaning with a dirty rag will make us clean. As my father was fond of saying, "you can't put perfume on a pig." If we want to rid ourselves of dirt, we must first admit to it . . . all of it.

Honesty – A Necessity for a Complete Cleaning

If we want a full cleaning, we can't do that in isolation, although we'd like to. Cleaning is a corporate activity. If we want an iridescently deep cleaning, we can only scrub out the deepest dirt with the scouring pad of a repentant attitude. That means we confess our dirt to those we harmed. We confess the wrongs, the behaviors, the choices, the attitudes, the selfishness, the intent to harm, the greed . . . we fess up and confess it. That's the scouring pad. Then we get on our hands and knees and take the detergent of honesty and accountability, and we clean. When we do that, we will live with lightness and vigor—not to mention a freedom that we could not have imagined.

Cleaning Requires Maturity

Many people walk around seeing themselves as shiny clean. We have this spit and polish attitude about ourselves. Yet, we're all dirty. Being dirty doesn't mean that we have to stay dirty. Being dirty doesn't mean that we're dirty people. It simply means that we're all fallen and that we all make mistakes. Bad choices are made in this world, and we make our fair share of them. Being accountable for our dirt and then rigorously cleaning it up allows the vibrancy and richness of our humanity to shine through and shine out. It maximizes who we are rather than forcing us to live a minimized life.

It allows for a transparency where we can intersect others and be intersected. And in the end, it just feels plain good. So, how about a deep clean?

CHAPTER 5

The New Year: Clean Slate or Simply Stale?

"Examine yourselves to see whether you are in the faith; test yourselves. Do you not realize that Christ Jesus is in you—unless, of course, you fail the test?"

—2 Corinthians 13:5

"No man was ever so much deceived by another as by himself."

—Fulke Greville

WITH EACH NEW YEAR, WE long for a fresh start. We want to wipe the slate clean, removing the muddy smudges and the mucky smears. We want to get rid of the errors, the poor choices, the misguided decisions, and the bruising flops that populated the previous year. We hope to wipe away old habits, clean up destructive behaviors, sponge up toxic relationships, run away from spirit-crushing jobs, and flee the debt-feeding financial decisions that we made. We desire to mop up the messes of failed relationships, torpedoed financial endeavors, underestimated obstacles, and overestimated abilities.

The New Year is our time to use a vigorous amount of elbow grease to clean up the messes of the old year. It's a time to sweep those dirty little choices under the carpet, smooth over places where the carnage of our decisions tore the landscape of our lives apart, and prop up the things that were blown over by the selfish choices we made. We patch it up, put it up, touch it up, roll it up, suck it up, wrap it up, and sometimes give it up. We're deeply engrossed in the "spit and polish" of getting everything tight and clean.

We desperately want to expunge the memory of the people we hurt from the recesses of our ever-annoying conscience, or we work hard to pretend that what we did wasn't really all that bad. We don't really want to acknowledge that we made incredibly stupid choices along the way—choices that had absolutely no foresight or hindsight. Instead, we write all the collateral damage off to the welcome scapegoat of misfortune, a tough economy, fate, chance, a fat chance, or the poor choices of others. We want to shake off the mishaps of the past year, rigorously brushing them off the sleeves of our lives so that they're left behind in the place we've been in order to be free of them in the place we're going. Such actions suggest our desperation for new beginnings and explain why God is the King of every new beginning.

THE PAST – RELISHED OR REJECTED?

We cross the threshold of the New Year without wanting to look back. It's not that we want to reject the past, but we much prefer to leave it behind. We want a clean break, a new beginning, a fresh opportunity that's in no way inhibited by whatever the past has been. Indeed, we do tend to cherish the good things that have happened. However, we seem to celebrate them with a diminished sense that they weren't as good as good can potentially be. We engage the New Year, holding out hope that it will bring us twelve months of living that will be good in a way that we haven't quite been able to achieve—that somehow this year will be what no year has yet been. So, celebration is often less about what we're leaving behind, and a whole lot more about what we hope will come.

THE MAGIC MIDNIGHT HOUR

Somehow, we presume that when the clock strikes 12:00 a.m. every January 1, there's some magical line of demarcation that we're finally allowed to cross. It's like waiting for the gates embedded in some wall to magically swing open at the stroke of twelve, granting us pell-mell passage into an entirely new place that we hope is indeed entirely new. In feverishly rushing through the gates with the massive hoard rushing right along with us, we've embraced a mentality that the bad stuff in our lives is forced to stay on the other side of those gates. We've developed a sense that something's shed, something's peeled away or purged from us in the passing. Once we've stepped across that line into the New Year, we've been cleansed and purified in the newness that represents the New Year. And because we have, we've likewise been granted a fresh, clean, and uninhibited new start.

We wouldn't necessarily verbalize these kinds of feelings. However, they're sufficiently embedded in humanity's deepest need to believe in the existence of new beginnings. We're desperate for new beginnings, but we tend to mar, scuff up, and sometimes obliterate the old ones.

THE SEEDS OF STALENESS

The New Year is the old year in redress. It's nothing more than the final tick of the second hand of the clock that throws December 31st over into January 1st. It leaves nothing old behind and takes nothing new with it. It's a continuation of whatever was, into whatever's going to be. There is no line of demarcation. If there is a line in it all, it's probably a less than desirable thread of continuity that we've relentlessly and probably thoughtlessly drawn across the threshold of every New Year and towed right through the heart of every day that followed it. There is nothing inherently new about New Year's.

Yet, because we ascribe a false newness to it, we assume that a habit or tendency has actually changed, that a weakness or label has really been left behind, that something has transitioned or transformed in the process of one day rolling into another. We unconsciously presuppose that we have been bathed in the purifying waters of a New Year. And we erroneously presume that if we carry any of the old over into the New Year, it's not because the old followed us but that we recreated it. If we're smart enough to realize that it's just another day, we're often not smart enough to realize that this new day doesn't afford us any more resources than yesterday did. Sometimes we see the New Year as handing us something new that we didn't have before. No such exchange transpires.

This falsely contrived sense leaves us with exactly the same stuff we had before the clock rolled over into a new day; yet we believe that somehow things have changed, or will magically change, or can change because we have some new resource. Out of that misguided assumption, we cast the bad, sour, and upsetting things of the past behind us, assuming that in the action of casting them behind us, they really are behind us. Yet, wanting something to be gone doesn't make it gone. Thinking we have some new resource doesn't actually put it into our hands.

So we celebrate, we "party", and we cause a raucous. We raise robust toasts to the new opportunities that we've fabricated from the broken and desperate shards of the past year. We pen feel-good resolutions across our minds and across the pages of the calendar of the upcoming year. We tell ourselves that it's going to be better, that we're going to beat old habits and turn careers around. We shout down the corridors of the New Year, declaring in advance that we're going to recommit to our marriages, that we're going to complete college degrees, balance our spending, drop those pounds, back off the alcohol, and watch our language. We assertively put the New Year on notice, telling it that we're going to beat addictions, spend wisely, change our attitudes, bury hatred, resurrect forgiveness, overcome fears, undercut bad attitudes, and basically *change*. Wow.

WIPING OUT STALENESS

The diamonds set deeply in all this is that every New Year is an opportunity for reflection. We've set the calendar and flow of the year in such a manner that the New Year is parked at a place that affords us perspective. Nothing changes. We've been handed nothing new. But we can stop, catch our breaths, rub our eyes clear of the debris that life scatters across them, brush off the dust that's caked on, and simply look around. We have a chance to inventory and assess, to engage the reality of our lives, evaluate those realities, execute strategies to change, and embrace an enthusiasm about the possibilities that these actions will bring to the New Year.

We can't wipe the slate clean, but we can rewrite it with the lessons of the past year. We won't be handed any new resource, and we won't be leaving anything behind, but we can develop new resources; we can systematically eliminate things from our lives so that they're eventually left behind. We can't ignore things, but we can change them. We can pretend that the New Year is something that it's not, or we can persevere in learning from the past in order to change the future.

The New Year does indeed present us with grand opportunities. But those are based in wise decisions shaped and fashioned from both the successes and failures of the previous year. We are afforded new beginnings, but not at the expense of the past being ruthlessly expunged or irresponsibly left withering in the trenches of the past year. There are precious lessons in the stench of failure and the filth of selfish choices. The new beginning is forged from the shards of the past, not from the abandonment of the past. So, start forging and make each year a truly new one.

CHAPTER 6

The Untimely:
When It All Happens
When It Shouldn't

"'For my thoughts are not your thoughts, neither are your ways my ways,' declares the LORD."

—Isaiah 55:8

"If you perceive that there are four possible ways in which a procedure can go wrong, and circumvent these, then a fifth way, unprepared for, will promptly develop."

—Unknown Author

SOMEONE ONCE UTTERED THE TIMELESS saying that "timing is everything." There's a calming feeling about things happening in a certain order in a certain time that makes it all fit in a certain way. We sense a natural and correct progression that, if followed, leads to success, happiness, fulfillment, or whatever it is that we're chasing. The whole element of timing seems critical. The more important things are, the greater the issue of timing seems to be. Timing can be so critical that at times we set out to minutely orchestrate the tiniest pieces and parts of all the many things that we're doing so that everything is perfectly cinched, tightly in synch, and precisely on time.

FALLING APART JUST TO FALL APART

Yet, sometimes it all falls apart anyway. I mean it disintegrates—something like Murphy's Law times three or four. Sometimes it's not just a matter of a relationship or a career being a bit out of step or not lining up quite right. It's not about tweaking a game plan that's abruptly turned south or gently nudging it back into the place it was supposed to be before it was abruptly derailed. Sometimes the wheels fall off the thing, which then causes everything else to fall off as well. We end up with the classic train wreck where we met a downhill train on an uphill grade. More than that, however, there's no rhyme or reason for the train wreck. It simply didn't need to be, but it was. It was all way beyond any odds or all statistics. Whatever happened, it was a cruelly extenuated string of stupid, dumb luck.

Sometimes it all falls apart….all of it. We're left standing dumbfounded, mired in the confusion of it all and running our minds down a thousand roads of the classic "what could have gone wrong?" question. Sure, we'll likely find some things that weren't well thought out or strategies that were a bit ill conceived. We might unearth some rationales that now, in hindsight, weren't quite as rational or shrewd as we originally thought them to be. We might stumble over some misdirected motivations or less than ethical agendas that were part of the whole thing. The way we pasted it all together may have not been seamless, and the stuff that we pasted together in the first place might have been less of a fit than we had originally thought. We may have even chosen to force fit some stuff that in the end really didn't mesh all too well. Yes, there are probably some quirks and a few flaws.

Yet, there are times when these quirks and flaws and other dynamics really represent only a small portion of the whole train wreck. We dig, scratch, and scrape only to uncover a sparse handful of these dynamics. There are times when the sum total of them is far too small and innocuous to explain why the wheels fell off and the whole thing fell apart. They don't add up sufficiently to explain the mess that lays scattered, derelict, smoking, and broken at our feet.

WHEN LACK OF TIMING MAKES US LOOK BAD

George McGovern once said, "You know, sometimes, when they say you're ahead of your time, it's just a polite way of saying you have a real bad sense of timing." Sometimes, we just try to play it all off or make light of it in order to make it lighter. We missed a step somewhere, we lost our place in the script, or we missed our cue. Now what? We can make it all cute and cut up about it. We can poke fun at ourselves to lighten everything up a bit. We can make polite statements to take the edge off our stupidity. But when we lose our timing and things go horribly wrong, there may be nothing remotely right that can be said.

NO ANSWERS

In the end, we're left with bushels of questions that rot for lack of answers. Things just didn't line up. There's no sustaining or compelling rationale other than it didn't happen when and how we expected. If the timing had been good, it all would have all been good. But the timing was not, and now everything lays wrecked and ravaged.

Sometimes, the losses are marginal. At other times, they're catastrophic. Sometimes, we can just pick up our toys, brush them off, head on home, and play another day. Sometimes, there's nothing left to pick up other than the charred ash of incinerated dreams and the unidentifiable pieces of years' worth of hope and sacrificial toil. Sometimes, it's no big deal, and at other times, the whole thing is a deal-breaker. Sometimes, we can pick up and move on, and at other times, there's nothing to pick up and no place to move on to.

BETTER QUESTIONS TO ASK

Maybe we should expand our thinking a bit. Maybe we should ask the question "is loss sometimes the best thing that can happen?" That's a bitter pill to swallow, on top of the fact that it's completely unsavory to even entertain in the first place. It suggests, however, that things in life don't line up because maybe they're not supposed to. Maybe what we were doing was a whole lot more wrong than it was right. Maybe it would have been a whole lot more damaging than it would have been constructive. Maybe it would have been the thing that robbed us blind rather than enriching us beyond measure. Maybe it would have become the monster rather than the benefactor. Maybe the fact that wheels fell off and it derailed was one of the biggest blessings we've experienced in a very long time.

Is there room in our thinking to entertain the possibility that failure is sometimes preferred to success? Success does not always deliver a blessing; failure does not always deliver a curse. Life is far too vast to place success and failure into the neat and tidy categories that we aptly apply in every situation. Sometimes, the best thing for us is the very thing that we feel is the worst thing. Sometimes, in God's grand scheme, pain and loss are the pavers to something grand and glorious. Sometimes, a misstep is a nothing more and nothing less than a change of cadence to right a path to God.

THE TAXING NATURE OF OUR PRECONCEIVED OUTCOMES

At the beginning, when we've started to head off into most of our endeavors, we don't have the perspective of what this will look like on the other end. All we see is what we have in front of us, how it all goes together, and then—based on that—how we guess it will all come out in the wash. We can take a shot at speculating outcomes and be convinced that our conceptualization will indeed be what it will look like on the other side. We can do the math and project the numbers and point to what it should all add up to. We can play with our mental bell-curves and crunch the emotional numbers to calculate an outcome. But sometimes things don't add up according to our calculations, despite how tedious they might be. Sometimes, our best projections become our most haunting nightmares.

We're typically not open to this kind of thinking because we're angry about the loss; we're licking our wounds because we feel cheated. We didn't land where we projected we would land, and we scour the minute fractions and infractions in order to get us to those ill-fated coordinates. We're not in the mindset to think that maybe it blew up so that we wouldn't. There's no room in our heads to realize that we might have just been saved from ourselves. We're too obstinate to realize that if we keep goading the situation in order to achieve our preconceived outcomes, there might come a point when we won't be saved from ourselves anymore. All we tend to focus on is the feeling that we've been victimized, ripped off, audaciously cheated, short-changed, and short-sheeted. The reality is that sometimes we are. But quite often, this is life's way of putting on the brakes.

Is It Untimely?

Are our circumstances untimely, or very timely? Do our situations appear untimely only because we're seeing what didn't happen? Do we refuse to see the things that are happening right in the middle of what didn't happen? Are we so myopic that we can't see beyond the train wreck to the fact that the wreck stopped the train and that this might have been the very thing that compassionately saved us or maybe graciously redirected us? To our chagrin, the exact time and place when we think something shouldn't have happened may very well be the exact time and place when it absolutely should have happened.

Rose Kennedy said, "Life isn't a matter of milestones but of moments." It's not about what we achieve but what we learn on the way to the achievement. We glue our eyes to the goal and ignore the journey on the way there. And that journey will often involve our world's falling apart despite heroic efforts to keep them together. Yet, our world's falling apart have within those events great lessons that we would be well advised to embrace. Moments are not always nice, but they can be rich. So, when your world falls apart in the untimeliness of living, look at the wreckage. You just may have been saved and didn't even know it. You just may have been mercifully redirected and missed it. Your world falling apart may in actuality be your world being put together.

CHAPTER 7

Sparrows in the Garage: Little Treasures

"But we have this treasure in jars of clay to show that this all-surpassing power is from God and not from us."

—2 Corinthians 4:7

"A box without hinges, key, or lid, yet golden treasure inside is hid."

—J.R.R. Tolkien

AN UNKNOWN AUTHOR WROTE, "REAL treasure lies not in what can be seen, but what cannot be seen." Oddly, we possess this absurd perception that we must be able to *see* something in order to treasure it. What we see as treasure is only the thing that's revealing the treasure itself. The treasure in a daisy is not the daisy, but the creative genius behind the daisy. The flower itself is simply a tender, fragrant, and quite intricate manifestation of the real treasure. Reflected in the wonder of this simple flower we are privileged to see is a whisper-thin slice of something truly marvelous. Real treasure lies nestled in hidden places with generous clues to its magnificence scattered all about like a generous field of daisies that rolls off to blue horizons. Sadly, we call those clues "treasure."

The real treasure is often too airy and intangible for us. But, we feel that we have to see treasure, which in reality keeps us from seeing treasure. Not only do we have to see treasure, we think that we have to be able to hold it in our hands. And then, in far too many cases, we think we have to be able to own it in order to treasure it. What we haven't figured out is that if we can possess some item, it's simply not a treasure, for real treasure is far too elusive to be held in the hands of any man.

Sadly, we rarely consider the reality that real treasure is the stuff that can't be seen. Therefore, we don't look for it because we presume that there's nothing to look for. Because we don't look for it, we miss real treasure and we accept the bogus, phony, plastic stuff of life for the stuff of treasure. We plod through life with our pockets crammed with a squalid array of worthless trinkets that we believe to be treasure. We live anemically impoverished lives—and we don't even know it.

In fact, it may well be that, to treasure something in a truly treasured manner, it must be entirely ethereal; it must be something that we can't see, that we can't hold, and that we can't own. When we possess something, the fact that we have the ability to possess it suggests that it's limited—so limited, in fact, that we can control it. Possessing something suggests that it's subject to our whims and the flux of our own whimsy. Anything we can control must have some sort of inferior status that automatically excludes it as being treasure of the most treasured sort.

Being unable to possess something suggests that it has a sweeping scope, an unfathomable significance, and a fathomless depth that is far beyond us—or beyond anyone else, for that matter. Real treasures are elusive because if they're not, they don't rise sufficiently above our sordid and stained humanity to be genuinely categorized as treasures. Real treasure will not be owned, bound, appraised, hemmed in, leashed, locked in a vault, confined to a trust, or be made subject to either our ridicule or praise. Real treasure is priceless because it supersedes and completely eclipses any rogue monetary standards that we'd foolishly attempt to place on it. Real treasure will not bow in servitude or obediently follow at our heels, because it is superior to us. Yet the real wonder of real treasure is that it is withheld from no one.

SPARROWS AND A CLAPBOARD GARAGE

Every spring, the sparrows came back to the old garage, like coming back to a comfortable, old friend. Darting and bouncing in feathered frenzy, they would burst from the muscular maples and the tangled brush of the mock orange bushes, flirting and flitting in front of the garage in some sort of grand hello after a winter's separation. Upon their return, their boundless energy and contagious enthusiasm seemed wildly intoxicating, vibrant, and filled with all the fresh energy of spring. I often wondered if they had spent the cold, gray months of winter in a nearly uncontrollable anticipation of greeting their old friend once winter had rolled off the horizon of spring.

Sometimes in life there seems to be a subtle yet wonderfully warm camaraderie of sorts that develops between things you'd never think would or could be connected like that. Those things are a kind of treasure in themselves. That seemed to explain the quiet, entirely unspoken kind of relationship that existed between the old garage and the sparrows. They seemed like old friends who didn't need to say much because the bond they shared spoke more than words ever could. The old clapboard garage and the house sparrows were each warmed, gently magnified, and beautifully enhanced by the other. Each was a treasure embraced as a treasure.

The sparrows would glide up between the heavy wooden doors and slip by the sturdy steel tracks that they ran on, seeming to nestle into the garage's soft, clapboard embrace. Every spring the sparrows would settle in and nest right above the heavy wooden doors, tucked just inside the thin edge of the garage attic. There was far too much love and warmth in the old garage, so there were usually two or three nests enfolded above the old wooden doors.

It was easy to see the sparrows coming and going as they bobbed and darted about. Yet, as with any real treasure, I couldn't see what they were doing. Treasure enveloped in secrecy always lends a bit of tantalizing mystery to it all. The sparrows were phenomenally tireless, transporting endless bits of straw and brown grasses into the garage, building a place to birth the treasures of the next generation. Within moments of entering the garage, they would poke out elated heads and then burst into flight with empty beaks. In no time, they would return with more strands of lacey grass, bits of tattered weed, cottony fibers, or limply discarded pieces of string . . . over and over.

Within weeks, the sound of new life could be heard tentatively reaching out from above the old, wooden doors. Scattered chirps and peeps liberally tossed out as brilliant rays of spring would be shushed when anyone approached. Patient mothers were teaching their little ones that life is an incomparable treasure, but treasure does not eliminate danger. These little, hidden treasures would become ever louder as they grew. They would grow strong and eventually seek the independence of flight. Before the close of spring, they would launch themselves in a gangly and awkward kind of flight. Curiosity would beckon them out to explore the places close to the garage, bursting into uncoordinated flight but never wandering too far way. Life would eventually call them out ever further from the clapboard garage until they were gone into summer's embrace.

CHARACTERISTICS OF TREASURES: UNOBTRUSIVE

Treasures are hidden away in quiet places. They speak in soft tones and often become silent as we approach. They don't beg to be found but embrace us if we do happen to find them. They are the product of completely ordinary circumstances unfolding in wonderfully extraordinary ways. They are found hidden in the nooks and crannies of our existence—all around us if we quit allowing our attention to be captivated by that which is noisy and listen for that which is quiet and still.

THE PRODUCT OF UNEXPECTED AND LOVING CAMARADERIE

Treasures are a product of treasures. Real treasure is the product of lives shared, experiences intermingled, roads merged into single lanes, sacrifices jointly experienced, the soulful laughter of two hearts in sync with each other, and lives bountifully expended in unity. Treasures are the stepchild of lives lived out in shared experiences that dramatically multiply both the experience and individuals in a manner geometrically beyond anything the individuals could hope to experience alone. Treasures rise out of the relationship of people who are intimately woven together by the threads of time and the needle of experience.

ALWAYS CREATING AND NEVER PRESERVING

Treasures are not stagnant. They're not to be preserved; in preserving, they will most certainly wither and perish. Real treasures begat other treasures. Real treasures are designed to perpetuate other treasures. Sometimes, the perpetuation involves the replication of the original treasure, and sometimes the replication is an object or relationship that's entirely different but just as wonderful. Treasures are ingenuously and deliberately crafted to enrich the world. If one thing is for certain, they are not designed to be encased in the lifeless museums of our making or the vaults we create to keep them to ourselves. It's in their multiplication that the cold of life's winters are forced off the edge of the calendar to make way for spring.

SOWN TO THE WORLD

It's our natural inclination to preserve treasures: to corral them, box them, and seal them tight. We assume that unless they're preserved, they'll be lost, which is contradictory. In fact, they are designed to be launched and thrown out to the horizons of each of our lives regardless of the season. Authentic treasures permeate our world; they gain wings of their own and disburse so that they might reproduce in other places and in other lives. The stuff of treasure is irrepressibly infectious and prudently wild, intent on providing enrichment whenever and wherever it can. We must work against our own inclinations and toss treasures out to the world around us.

It would be wise to rethink the concept of treasure in your own life. What you may be holding onto may not be treasure at all. In fact, if you're "holding" onto it, it's not.

CHAPTER 8

Our Metronome: Timing

"There is a time for everything, and a season for every activity under the heavens: a time to be born and a time to die, a time to plant and a time to uproot, a time to kill and a time to heal, a time to tear down and a time to build."

—Ecclesiastes 3:1-3

"The early bird gets the worm, but the second mouse gets the cheese."

—Willie Nelson

HENRY DAVID THOREAU WROTE THE classic quote, "If a man loses pace with his companions, perhaps it is because he hears a different drummer. Let him step to the music which he hears, however measured, or far away." The assumption in Thoreau's statement is that life is far too wonderful and comparatively too vast to have it all march to a singularly stale drumbeat. Despite our inclination to demand one drumbeat, there are many.

Indeed, all of life is lived walking to some sort of cadence that keeps us all moving forward in a joint journey from here to a better place. There's a persistent drumbeat that nudges us to keep on moving when our own rhythm has been lost in our own lost-ness. There's a drumbeat that gives us a reliable and incessantly invigorating rhythm by which to keep moving when we can't keep in step with anything. There's a drumbeat that taps out the reality that there's something ahead when we can't see anything ahead or behind. There's a drum-beat that pounds out the promise of another place other than this one. There's a drumbeat that says it's not over, it's not the end, and everything is just a step to something else if we just keep stepping.

That drumbeat is a bit different for each of us. To erase the full-ness of its vast chords and strip it down to a single naked notation, to peel away the variety of measure and shackle it with iron chains to a single shrill beat, to do these things would make us a world of automatons marching in lock step to nothingness. As Thoreau said, "If a man loses pace with his companions, perhaps it is because he hears a different drummer." How marvelous is that kind of variety.

A Metronome Gone Lost and Stale

We all have a sense of timing—a metronome that's setting the cadence of our lives. All of us are marching to some tempo of some sort, some beat that's set by some device in our lives. Typically, we've become so accustomed to the signal that it becomes nothing more than "white noise": that thing that we've heard so much that we don't consciously hear it anymore. It's there, it's regular, it's regulated, it keeps ticking off some sort of rhythmic beat, and we keep right on walking to it. Yet, because it's methodically recurring, it becomes that invisible white noise that we don't hear any longer. So we presume it's not there.

Setting Our Cadence by the Beat of the World

We like to think that we're freer than that. We prefer to entertain the delusion that we can change up our cadence whenever we want to, in whatever way we want to change it. Beyond that, we want to believe that we have the ability to blatantly ignore every drumbeat and skip through life with some sort of "in-your-face" anarchy.

In fact, at times we're pompous enough to believe that there is no drummer at all and that we're playing it entirely by ear. Forget the whole drummer thing. We feel that we live in a world that unflinchingly declares that we have the freedom to change up our cadence at a moment's notice. Life moves fast. Life moves in unpredictable currents and can change its direction with a single decision, a sole event, or one swipe of the second hand. Because it can, we can't be bound by some pathetically regulated and irritatingly monotonous beat that drones on at exactly the same tempo despite the always-changing tempo of the world around us.

It's Up Us to Set Our Cadence

Since that's the case, we have to set the cadence. Get rid of the drum, burn the drumsticks—or use them as chopsticks the next time we're out for Chinese food. Our goal is to set our ear to ground and determine the ever-changing tempo of the world. We must be razor-sharp, wise, and sage-like. We have to be incessantly discerning, always having our finger directly on the pulse of the world so that we can mimic it in perfect timing. We have to know the precise rhythm of the world so that we're not rhythmically left behind.

We find that mimicking the rhythm of the world is too simple and insufficient. We need to determine what the rhythm of the world is and then determine how we're going to position ourselves in reference to that rhythm. Sometimes that means we're going to set our rhythm a bit slower or a bit faster. We might change it up a bit or simply walk in step with the cadence of the world. All of that depends on our chosen strategy. That strategy is usually designed to get us wherever the world's going—ahead of the world getting there. Or, we want to get to the same place the world's going to at the same time it's going to arrive there, but we want to arrive at that place a lot better off or with a lot more stuff than the world will have when it gets there. But all of this is based on the belief that we set our own cadence.

THE METRONOME

There's a spiritual core to us that sets a universal cadence. We're unable to walk through life without some sort of beat to walk to. Despite our own headiness, we're not good enough to keep changing it up as the beat around us keeps changing up. None of us are deft enough to prance through this existence with the ability to hear every tone, every nuance, every note, and every beat along the way. The songs are far too prolific, the beats are far too diverse, the rhythms are far too varied, and the alterations that inevitably happen to all of them occur before we're able to figure out what the last one was. Navigating the world today and trying to figure out what our cadence should be is something akin to being a drummer playing for a dozen different bands that are playing a dozen different songs at the exact same time. You just can't do it.

WHO OR WHAT SETS OUR METRONOME?

We all have a metronome. The larger question is: who sets it? We can presume that we do. That assumption implies that we have the resources to set it in a world that's so big and is changing so fast that we can hear it all and adjust to it all. If we run on that assumption, we'll never quite be in step. We might be close at times. However, the odds are that we'll be pretty much off beat and largely out of tempo. And that can look downright ugly and be outright embarrassing.

WHAT REALLY SETS THE CADENCE?

It seems that we think that the cadence of the world is set by the world that we see. Such a perspective reveals our minimalist and myopic view of the world. What we see is only a minute part of all that exists. Simone de Beauvoir wrote, "I am incapable of conceiving infinity, and yet I do not accept finity." If we are finite in an infinite world, then we represent such a microscopic part of it that we're nearly indiscernible in the mass of it. If that's the case, we don't set the metronome, nor do any of the things that we see. What sets the metronome of our world is something more vast and more expansive than we are.

Therefore, whatever sets the metronome has to be something that understands, embraces, and effectively incorporates a world that's running wild and in crazily sporadic patterns. Whatever sets our metronome can't and won't set the cadence based on the cadence of the world. It must set it to something superior to our world. It must supersede the world, be above the world and beyond the world. It can't match the tempo of the world because that tempo is not a tempo at all. Rather, the tempo of the world is chaos and confusion marching in a million directions all at once. The metronome of the world is nothing more than a tempo that's designed to keep everything from falling apart. It's like someone riding a bike for the first time. The goal isn't to ride the bike. The goal is to keep from falling down. That's the world, and the world constantly falls off the bike.

I think that we want a whole lot more than simply a goal of not falling down. We need to be attentive and obedient to the tempo of a metronome that isn't based on the erratic tempo of a world trying not to fall. That metronome won't be found in the world. It's found above, beyond, outside, and yet squarely in the world all at the same time. It supersedes the world and yet is woven throughout the whole fabric of the world. It is both totally the world and totally not the world. It can completely understand the world and yet look beyond the world to see everything that's beyond it. It understands that the cadence of the world is set by factors outside of the world. If we can find something like that, we can rest in its tempo. We need to seek that metronome and be obedient to its tempo.

THE METRONOME OF GOD

God pounds out the cadence that all of eternity walks to. That cadence is clearly heard in the cellular structure of a single blade of grass, and it's heeded by muscular galaxies that embrace expanses light years in width. That rhythm was tapped out into a brand new creation flailing in confusion where God gently called order out of chaos at creation. Chaos was made to be ordered. Once chaos was channeled and culled into rhythmic step, a world of marvel and majesty emerged. God takes our chaos and sets it to His cadence. When that happens, our chaos turns to marvel and majesty. It's walking to His drumbeat. It's being attuned to that rhythm. It's being obedient to the drummer of all drummers. When we walk in that kind of step, we're walking in wonder to wonder. Stop and listen for the drumbeat of God. It's there, it's the perfect cadence for now, and it will walk us in perfect step right into the embrace of eternity.

SECTION TWO

Simple Truths for Profound Relationships

CHAPTER 9

Fight or Flee: Our Contradictory Nature in Crisis

"You will not have to fight this battle. Take up your positions; stand firm and see the deliverance the LORD will give you, Judah and Jerusalem. Do not be afraid; do not be discouraged. Go out to face them tomorrow, and the LORD will be with you [emphasis mine]."
—2 Chronicles 20:17

"Fight or flight? If I had wings, there'd be no choice. But since I don't have wings, I have to rely on my cape, and a long running start."
—Jarod Kintz

THE SAYING IS THAT "IT comes in threes." Whether things actually come in sets of three or not is debatable. However, the principle that things often happen in clusters or come in bunches often holds true. How or why that happens is part of the curious alchemy of life. As things quite often go, when we're hit, we're usually hit by more than one thing at a time. Sometimes we're hit so incredibly hard by one thing that we can't conceptualize that anything else could possibly hit us. You would think that there would be a point where life would look upon us with a pinch of sympathy and a dollop or two of empathy and say enough is enough. There's a deep feeling that justice and fairness would reign in anything else that might happen to us . . . but something else happens anyway.

We've probably all had the experience where the assaults seem relentless, something akin to another saying that goes "when it rains, it pours." If it were just rain, it might not be so bad. But more often than not, the things that hit us are nothing like rain at all. Rather, they are like tornados of horrific proportions or hurricanes that are way beyond anything natural and more like something evil and savage.

The "Why" Versus the "What"

When things happen to us in clusters and come in bunches, we're often thinking less about the specific things that are happening and more about why they're happening all at once. It becomes a whole lot larger than that. It becomes an issue of why life works the way it sometimes does rather than how life plays itself out in the specific details. We lose the focus on *what* happened and become consumed by *why* it happened. As often happens when we focus on the why, we lose our grounding; focusing on the why doesn't solve the what. So our wailing cries for justice obscure what the injustice was all about.

I think that most of us have come to understand that "life happens" and that sometimes it happens in ways that are not only tough but outright vicious. We all know that life can be an arrogant bully. It can make the choice not to play by our rules. We know that there's a strong probability that, at the absolute worst time, life will run entirely contrary to what we think is right and run right over us. Life is not fair. We know that factually, but we haven't embraced that emotionally. There's something about life pooling a collection of bad stuff together and dropping it on us all at once that takes us beyond what we perceive to be the natural stuff that happens in life. We end up with a sense that life has become completely unfair and far too difficult, so difficult that our very survival can come into question.

OUR RESPONSE TO CRISIS

When life hits us like that, it tends to elicit within us two entirely contradictory feelings. One is a sense of rebellion that rallies us to rise and fight the things that have befallen us. There's that sense that we want to fight back and throw back at life what it's thrown at us. It's a core response of righteous rebellion where we act because we feel an injustice has happened, and our action is about bringing justice to whatever the injustice has been. Sometimes such an atrocious injustice has been perpetrated upon us that any fear that we have is completely bulldozed by our furious need to retaliate. The emotional response is so strong that we can rise up with incredible determination.

The other response is a sense of hopelessness that prompts us to throw up our hands in abject surrender and walk away or, worse yet, question if we can survive at all. Sometimes the greatest energies that we can call up, the most profound strength that we can assimilate and bring to bear is simply not enough. We can call up all the assets that we have within us and pull together all of the resources around us, and with it all collected, realize that we just don't have enough to cope. There are times when life hits us so hard that everything that we can gather together is simply inadequate. It's here at these times we become frighteningly desperate because we realize that there's nothing left and there's no backup. There's a feeling that is hauntingly debilitating when we see no way out and no resource to get us out.

We tend to swing between these two extremes on some sort of long-drawn emotional pendulum. At times we buck up, thrust out our chests in some sort of confident defiance, and rush forward. At other times, we're discouraged and sheepish, finding our energies sapped and our motivation shot. We sometimes fight, and we sometimes flee. Most of the time, we're not certain why we're doing either. It's the oddity of facing the very same situation, confidently believing in ourselves at some points, and having no belief in ourselves at others.

THE PERSISTENCE OF BELIEF

Bruce Springsteen said, "Some guys, they just give up living, others start dying little by little, piece by piece, some guys come home from work and wash up, and go racing in the streets." It's about getting up again. It's about being relentless when it feels that it's entirely impossible to be relentless. There are times when we can't visualize a successful outcome, so we stop reaching out for one. When life hits us many times at the very same time, we lose a sense that time can heal anything at all. An outcome of some sort seems entirely unfeasible and wholly improbable, so we let ourselves die little by little.

These are the times when we need to act solely on a belief in an outcome, despite the fact that we can't even see the faint shadow of some faint outcome. We work toward what we cannot see, knowing that seeing is not a prerequisite as to whether something exists or not. Beliefs means putting some pretty heavy stock in what we can't yet get our hands on. It means that we refuse to live with the frailness of needing to hold some object or relationship in order to believe in it. The persistence of belief means that everything that would tell us that we're foolish for believing is itself foolish for not believing.

THE PERSISTENCE OF LIFE

Life cannot be judged on a sense of fairness. Life can and will be unfair. There's a basic need to embrace that reality so we don't spin, sputter, and throw up our hands in surrender when it is unfair. When we get slammed, we don't have to pout, pick up our toys, and run home. Instead, we do exactly the opposite: we persist. Persistence isn't scrupulously weighed out by applying some tedious equation that's dictated by the obstacles that unfairness tosses in front of us on the racetrack of our lives. Persistence is plenty smart enough to realize life will be unfair. Persistence is sufficiently wise enough to take the reality of unfairness into full consideration and decide to give it no consideration. Persistence is frankly realistic enough to take unfairness to task in order to complete any task.

THE PERSISTENCE OF OPPORTUNITY

Regardless of what life does to us and how it does it, there's always opportunity in it—always. If there's anything just about all of this, it's that there is always, always opportunity for growth and maturation, regardless of what hits us. We may wish to forfeit all of that because we'd prefer to avoid pain, and in order to do that, we'd gladly give up the growth. But guess what! We can't forfeit the pain, because it's not within our power to determine if most things are going to happen to us or not. So we might as well ask the larger, dramatically bolder question of what's the growth in this for us, because it's there every time.

Bill Watterson said, "I know the world isn't fair, but why isn't it ever unfair in my favor?" The reality is that unfairness is always fair in terms of what kind of growth it can bring to our lives. Outwardly, the circumstances and situations can be entirely and irrevocably unfair. The unfairness blocks our vision to see anything else but the unfairness. Yet, the invisible fairness in it all is that there is always opportunity for remarkable growth. More than that, the way things play is that if we're willing to look past the unfairness and look for the growth, the growth is such that it can be decadently superior to the pain that created the opportunity for the growth. We just don't see it because we're consumed with the unfairness; we're caught in the dramatic swing of our emotional response to it, and we can't see an outcome in the dust and wreckage.

THE OUTCOME OF RESTING IN BELIEF, LIFE AND OPPORTUNITY

Rather, we need to rest in the persistence of belief that there is an outcome somewhere, the Persistence of Life that things happen and we need to accept that they do, and the absolute Persistence of Opportunity that tells us that the growth in it all far exceeds any pain. Embrace these things and our nature in crisis will not be to flee. Instead, it will always be one where we forge forward, press outward, and climb upward. The results of these are a life of momentum, purpose, intentionality, and power. That's a great life indeed.

CHAPTER 10

Loneliness: Agendas that Starve Relationships

"Whoever winks with their eye is plotting perversity; whoever purses their lips is bent on evil."

—Proverbs 16:30

"So, I'm lying on the couch and Laura walks in and I say, 'Free at last,' and she says 'You're free all right, you're free to do the dishes.' So I say, 'You're talking to the former president, baby,' and she says, 'consider this your new domestic policy agenda.'"

—George W. Bush

WE LIVE OUR LIVES BASED on agendas. Most of our agendas are pretty subdued so that we don't often recognize them or comprehend exactly how they affect our behaviors and our choices. Those hidden agendas subtly ooze out in the living out of our lives, which makes them less than hidden and more unacknowledged. On the other hand, some of our agendas are glaring, screaming into our lives in a manner that every action and choice is methodically dictated by them. Demanding or demur, we all have agendas that have a firm hand in dictating what we do.

Agendas have a methodical way of commandeering our thinking. They can create within us an ever-increasing sense that if we don't adhere to them, we're going to be in big trouble. While agendas may start out innocently as goals or frameworks that are designed to productively channel various aspects of our lives, they often grow to monolithic proportions. Sometimes our agendas become tyrannical gods, legalistic rules, incessantly demanding expectations or rock-hard boundaries that are held as imperative. Our agendas can grow to behemoth proportions, ruthlessly demanding our obedient adherence and complete surrender as some sort of milk-toast vassal. At their most egotistical extremes, our agendas demand that we bow in abject worship of them as an end-all god of some kind. We then *become* our agendas, and we subsequently project our agendas into everything we touch.

Agendas and Relationships

Because of the intimacy and vulnerability of relationships, agendas tend to rear their ugly heads with quite a bit of force in most of our relationships. Agendas in relationship tend to turn bad because they're typically self-centered. Agendas are often distilled from the sour ingredients of our own self-centeredness. Those agendas poured into relationships will only result in a tone and flavor that sets our teeth on edge and ends in gross disappointment.

Most relationships don't start out that way, but as they evolve, so does the implementation and integration of our agendas. In time, our agendas become the things that define the relationship rather than the people in the relationship. There's a dictatorial sense to it; a suffocating and strangling kind of orientation where people are made to fit each other's agendas. The relationship itself is thoroughly stifled and ends up pooling in the rank waters of relational stagnation. In time, the relationship can become intolerable and even toxic. At that point, it's vacated because it's become insufferable.

There are a number of agendas that we forcefully cram into relationships—or cram relationships in to. If there's one thing that's for certain, certain agendas are certain to kill a relationship. In doing an agenda inventory of our relationships, we may want to look for some of these:

THE AGENDA OF POWER AND LEVERAGE

Typically, we build relationships to build out our goals. Relationships often become little more than a resource to be toyed with for our gain. Often, the ultimate objective is to use the relationship to achieve the goal we have in mind. Relationships are seen as a tool, some sort of asset, a connection that gives us power or leverage. Sometimes, we see it as the thing that supplies us with strength or motivation when we're expended, or as a resource that undergirds us when our energies flag and our fears flare. It's that thing we can fall back on when we need a boost, the thing we turn to when our emotional legs buckle, or the thing that lends some degree of accountability and causes us to "buck up" when we're burning out. Whatever we use it for and wherever it fits, it becomes an egocentric resource rather than relationship. It becomes two people being together for the benefit of one.

To view a relationship as a connection to be used is to insure its death. When a relationship dies, a bit of us dies with it. In that sense, using a relationship for our advantage is clearly using it for our disadvantage—not to mention that the other person doesn't fare all that well either. Relationships need to be fed and nurtured with ample space to allow them to flourish. Power and leverage too often become punitive and lethal.

THE AGENDA OF "BECAUSE WE'RE SUPPOSED TO"

Of course, we're supposed to have friends. And because we're supposed to have them, we'd better go out and round up a few of them.

After all, we wouldn't want to look like social misfits, undesirables, or people who live on the fringe of society and have people look at us sideways. So we have to claim knowledge of somebody or that we hung out with so-and-so. Sometimes relationships are what we're supposed to have in order to look the part, and so we go out and we collect them. It's like playing "dress up," where we put on people like some kind of finery and strut about with an air of importance and social finesse. It's the "look at me" scenario: "ain't I something?"

People are not clothing, nor are they some sort of fashion accessory. They're not points to be counted as we tally up our social scoreboard. They're not steps on some sort of social ladder, nor are they an aphrodisiac for our insecurities. Relationships are not about what we're supposed to do, but who we're supposed to be in a relationship where we elevate another in lieu of elevating ourselves. Any other agenda kills relationships.

The Agenda of Working Out My Issues

We all have issues. Sometimes we view relationships as the place where we can work out our issues. There's some sort of belief that the person we're in the relationship with will have some sort of ability to help us navigate our issues. It could be that they're close to us, that we see them as committed to us, or that we can be vulnerable with them in ways we can't with others. We sometimes believe that relationships are all about helping everyone become the best that they can be, that they create a place to maximize oneself, that they contain the ingredients for health that you won't find by being out there alone. Relationships are viewed as a sauna, a therapist, a good massage, and a room full of "warm and fuzzy" paraphernalia all mixed together. Then it's seasoned with a generous pinch of feel-good experiences thrown in for good measure.

Relationships are sometimes seen as having this emotionally magical thing going on. All we've got to do is lightly sprinkle this relational fairy dust on ourselves long enough and—abracadabra—we're good. Relationships are sometimes seen as the place to heal our issues.

While healing can certainly take place, inherently a relationship does not possess everything that we need to heal everything in our lives. Nor is a relationship to be constricted by such myopic thinking.

THE AGENDA OF REVENGE

Maybe we're in a relationship to get back at someone else. The relationship we're in is about revenge, about throwing something in someone's face who hurt us previously. At times, the relationship we're engaged in has little or nothing to do with the person we're in the relationship with. The relationship itself is in actuality targeting someone entirely outside the relationship. It's about retribution for a perceived hurt that was inflicted or a harm done. Maybe it's purely about manipulation as we attempt to press our agendas with someone else through the relationship that we're in. A relationship can be all about throwing someone else under the proverbial bus, about fueling the flames of jealousy in another, or simply strutting our stuff by having someone else hanging on our arm.

Other times, it's our way to break with another person or an entire social grouping by aligning ourselves with somebody who's completely removed from them. We may need a new, clearly defined beginning. So a new relationship may give detailed clarity and clear-cut definition in our break from an old lifestyle, an old flame, an old social circle, an old belief system, or an old goal.

WHAT'S YOUR AGENDA?

Maybe you never thought about your agendas. They become such a natural part of our thinking that we don't even see them as agendas anymore. They will have the toxic impact that so many agendas have in relationships. Think about yours. Think about their legitimacy. Think about the agenda of your agendas. Think about where they come from and where they ultimately take you. And most importantly, ask if you really want to keep them.

CHAPTER 11

Loneliness: Communication that Starves Relationships

"Therefore confess your sins to each other and pray for each other so that you may be healed."

—James 5:16

"Speak when you are angry – and you'll make the best speech you'll ever regret."

—Dr. Laurence J. Peter

LIFE IS A JOURNEY, AND it's anything but a solo one. Living is a voyage of companionship. But far more than that, along the journey and deep within the voyage, we find richness in relationships with those who know us intimately in a manner that can obliterate the terrifying sense of aloneness and wipe out the crippling sense of meaninglessness. There's an indefinable camaraderie in relational intimacy that lends a priceless and terribly rare sense of meaning to the journey. Relationships infuse the journey with an often surprisingly exuberate strength. They are the tightly braided netting that supports us along the way and catches us when we fall. Relationships are indispensable.

We desperately need those who can share in the muddy rigors and turbulent turmoil of our journey in a manner that expands the meaning and the joy of the journey in ways we hadn't even thought of at the outset. There is a privileged sort of strength where two souls firmly braided together are far more than the sum total of two souls who never merge. To journey alone is to journey to possible success. But to journey alone is to journey to success that is empty, pitifully vacant, likely isolating, and therefore void of the sense of success despite the success itself.

WHAT IS INTIMACY?

Life is a journey, and it's not a solo one. It's designed for intimacy. So what's real intimacy? Raw intimacy is that soul mate kind of connection that has nothing to do with physical intimacy. Real intimacy has everything to do with the complexity of two human beings finding a fundamental interweaving of their corporate humanity that together renders them more than the sum of whomever or whatever they are apart. It's the realization that I'm alone in this life as single human being whose experience is uniquely mine. My experiences are limited to my experience, but they are enlarged when they are brought into fellowship with the experience of another.

As part of the odd mystery of it all, we're individual people in a world that affords us the opportunity of intimacy. We can be a single entity within a corporate entity. We have the privilege of taking the unique experience that is exclusively ours and connecting every trace of that experience with another human being. If done with selflessness and a meticulous commitment to the relationship, that unification can result in the loss of none of our uniqueness whatsoever, instead bringing a wonderful magnification of that uniqueness. In the magic of our humanity, this kind of relationship can expand both people beyond the sum total of whomever they are as individuals. Such a convergence results in sweet undercurrents that meld the tributaries of two people, leaving aloneness to drown in those sweet waters.

Relationships enrich. They are a gift, an opportunity, the creation of a wildly imaginative God who wanted us to have everything that we are and enjoy the "everything" of another human being with the ability to have each enriched beyond measure. Relationships expand us. Relationships always have some critical element to add when everything else in life has nothing left to add to us. Relationships touch lonely souls, dust off our dispirited spirits, feed starving hearts, and lift faltering minds. They expand our horizons and embolden our hopes.

But we can't have relationships if we can't communicate. If you take communication out of relationships, you have no relationship; it's that simple. Communication is essential, yet we're losing the very ability to communicate.

LONELINESS AND FULL IN-BOXES

Loneliness is about relationships or, more fundamentally, the absence of relationships. The word *relationship* has become ill-defined or under-defined in a culture that consistently moves in wildly random directions at speeds that we can't even begin to define—other than to say that whatever speed it is, it's not fast enough. Relationships are cultured in the generous hands of time. They're nurtured in the warm folds of patient hearts that realize that the sweeping second hand of time cannot provide any kind of measure for relationships. Relationships are rigorously held apart from imprisoning task-oriented mindsets, and they're held in the listless hands of nurture—hands that are flagrantly and comfortably generous with time.

Because of the speed in which we're relentlessly moving, we communicate just enough to fill the informational void, get the data, plug it in, or meet some brief connective need of the moment so that we can move on to the next moment to make room for the moment that comes after that. George Bernard Shaw wrote, "The single biggest problem in communication is the illusion that it has taken place." The acquisition of data and the obtaining of information convey some bit of information, but that's *not* communication. It does, however, leave us with the abysmal illusion that communication took place, yet it's illusion only. We're left with a bunch of data and an equally engulfing sense of aloneness. Data does not a relationship make.

All the while, we're attempting to connect, build relationships, and maintain relationships in the snippets, sound-bites, and precariously thin threads of texting, posting on walls, blogging, connecting with our "tweets," IM'ing, and so forth. We have electronic communication that fires messages at the speed of light to devices half a world away or to the cell phones hanging on our hips. We can Skype and utilize a prolific array of web cams that splash images across screens that emblazon it all in the vividness of HD.

Sure, these modes of communication provide for the transmission of data. But they're not sturdy enough or sufficiently deep enough, and they don't possess the essence of the human touch adequately enough to connect with the heart and soul of another human being. Certainly, these types of communication have their place. But they fall short and are woefully inadequate in connecting the beating heart and tender spirit of one human being to another. They are incapable of weaving together the fabric of two complex souls so that they can fully share in the human journey in a divinely unified partnership.

Relationships are about the degree of connectivity that we have with others. Degree implies depth, that kind of connection that's calibrated by ever-deepening degrees of intimacy that bonds us in a cement-like fashion with another. Sure, we can have a boatload of acquaintances; we can be social butterflies that flit and flirt around a never-ending array of people in a completely shallow, flirtatious dance. We can play the social games and do the various gatherings and have everyone think that we're so wonderful and so clever and so quick and so charming and so brilliant. We can be the life of the party.

But that's an orchestrated show designed to impress. In the end, everyone walks away entertained, having had a rollicking good time, but with nothing other than a perpetuated sense of emptiness. After we digest all the entertainment, we're left wondering whether there are any real people out there. What those kinds of interactions are not is an honest interaction stripped intentionally bare by vulnerability. The sole intent of an honest interaction is to engender nothing but the most undiluted intimacy with another human being who feels as empty and lonely as we do.

COMMUNICATION AS CRITICAL

Communication is the bridge by which two lives intersect. It's a communion of souls, a bathing in the heart of another, a melding of two people into one while the individuals stay uniquely themselves. It's about seeing in and seeing through another soul that ultimately allows us to step into the very intimacy and indescribable marvel of that soul. This is not about data transmission or sharp sound-bites. It's not about how many gigabytes we've used or what we used them for. It has nothing to do with data streams or encryption. Communication is the use of words, intonation, touch, body language, eye contact, actions, behaviors, and so much more that is the stuff of the human soul. The stuff of the soul is not transmittable by any electronic device.

Phyllis McGinley wrote, "Sticks and stones are hard on bones, aimed with angry art, words can sting like anything, but silence breaks the heart." We can say a lot of things and make a lot of noise, but how many times is what we're saying nothing more than silence? How many times do we think we're communicating when all we're doing is conveying information—relational silence? Your relationship will not survive on the conveyance of information, despite how adept you might be at it. Your relationship can only survive on communication—sacredly intimate, foundationally core, and wholly heart marinated communication. So you would be well advised to consider whether you're conveying information and living in relational silence, or if you're communicating. There's a world of difference that will dictate the world of your relationships.

CHAPTER 12

Loving Your Enemies: More Than a Nice Idea

"But love your enemies, do good to them, and lend to them without expecting to get anything back. Then your reward will be great, and you will be children of the Most High, because he is kind to the ungrateful and wicked."

—Luke 6:35

"The best way to destroy an enemy is to make him a friend."
—Abraham Lincoln

LIFE HAS THOSE LINGERING PROVERBIAL statements that seem timeless, those quips and quotes that have an irresistibly compelling message. Whatever they might say, they say something that's so core to us or who we'd like to be that, secretly, we'd love to be able to live them out. It seems that because they have something genuinely real to them, they persist indefinitely because they're fresh and applicable.

However, it seems that these timeless, proverbial treasures are so good that they're too good to be true, or least too good to be achievable. We'd love to be able to actually do what they say and live like they suggest, but they're demanding and downright rigorous. In fact, they're sometimes so demanding and rigorous that they seem impossible. We have this curious way about us where we can conjure up truly great ideas that are so great that we can't seem to achieve them. Yet, they remain compelling, like some precious gem just beyond our reach.

Love Your Enemies

The command to love our enemies is clearly one of those messages. It certainly sounds nice. It sounds right. Intellectually, it's solid. It's principled. It would probably relieve a lot of our stress. It would likely make the world that "kinder, gentler" kind of place. It would probably diffuse a whole lot of stuff and smooth over things before any real damage is done. Forgiving our enemies would change the entire complexion of situations that looked pockmarked, potholed, and pitted. It would release anger, reorient attitudes, and restore whatever had been destroyed in whatever the situation might have been. Forgiving our enemies releases us, releases them, and restores the agitated landscape of our lives to peace and calm. Indeed, it is immensely powerful.

How Realistic is That?

Yeah, but how realistic is that command? Face it; we live in the twenty-first century. Look around. It's not a "kinder, gentler" kind of world. Rather, it's a place where we need to be on our guard and protect ourselves, or we're eventually going to be "ground round" in some situation with someone sooner or later. Someone in some way is going to coming gunning for us, whether in some subtle or some blatantly rancid kind of way. We're going to take a jab, get a bomb dropped on us, or have the rug pulled out from under us. We live in a world that's not shy about slicing and dicing us up if given the chance.

Taking that thinking a bit further, how do we forgive the people who intentionally beat us up in any number of ways? Is loving these people even remotely reasonable? That line of thinking seems to imply that we're somehow granting their actions a degree of permission or legitimacy. Aren't we telling the offender that their offenses are okay? Are we handing them a free pass to take another jab at us?

It seems to suggest that we're up for further offenses, that we've become the proverbial doormat in that relationship. How do we love in a world that doesn't understand love and will in all likelihood read the action of love in a way that's immature, naïve, passive, or just plain stupid? Loving then means wantonly setting the stage and orchestrating the situation in a way that's sure to result in a production of great personal calamity. Why do that?

Oscar Wilde said, "Always forgive your enemies—nothing annoys them so much." That sounds appealing in a sneaky way because that's really about a covert kind of revenge. In actuality, that's more a sinister way of getting back at our offenders without them really knowing that we're getting back at them. We can love in a way that backhands people and leaves them reeling without knowing what just hit them. We can play that game and call it love, but that's not about love.

THE COST TO OUR ENEMIES

What we don't consider is the cost our enemies pay in being exactly that: our enemies. Being our enemy demands that a person do things or carry out certain actions that make him or her our enemy in the first place. Our enemies are not enemies without some sort of decision or action that makes them our enemies. Something was done to us, some event transpired, or some situation was initiated that clearly put them in a starkly adversarial position. In other words, they had to do something to become our enemies.

And that action had to be severe enough to rupture, smash, or entirely decimate our relationship. Their actions had to be sufficiently toxic to set them completely at odds with us. Some significant action or choice had to transpire to polarize our relationship with them and put us at the opposite ends of the spectrum in some sort of adversarial stand-off. Something very bad had to have been done by our enemy.

What we think about is the cost of that action to us. In fact, we tend to be all about that. We can easily and quite extensively tell people how bad it was, how much it hurt, how unfair it was, and how uncalled for the actions were. We can cry the tears and magnify everything under the enlarging lens of drama. We can pound our fists and rail against horrific offenses that bespeak the evil character of the offender. We can recite all of that with great ease and theatrical flair.

What we don't think about is the cost of that behavior to our enemy. Of course we don't. We probably don't have much interest in going over that; we'd prefer to lick our wounds in light of the abuses that were perpetrated upon us. The abuses levied against us get all of our attention and the majority of our emotional airtime. It's not that we shouldn't deal with those things. We should. The problem is that they become our sole focus.

We can't forget that doing these things to us comes with a stiff cost to the person who's doing them. In fact, it's likely that the cost to our enemies for the things that they've done to us or against us is greater than the cost of those actions upon us. We don't see the cost to our enemies, because we're the ones in pain. We assume that the level of pain we're experiencing reflects the cost, and it's likely that our enemy is not in pain. In fact, they might be downright happy and somewhat elated about what they've done to us. They may have had a jolly good time ripping us apart. It may have been all raucous fun for them.

However, there are consequences for how we live our lives—deep, profound, and devastating consequences. Many times, those consequences aren't reflected in the pain someone is experiencing, and they're not necessarily reflected in whatever the outcome of the moment is. Most consequences are much deeper, feeling more like a slow acidic burn that gradually eats away at the edges of our souls, killing us in small degrees. There's a conscience ignored that will eventually have its day. There's the reality that nothing's ever done in isolation and that when anyone sows pain or betrayal or abandonment or rejection or any other destructive thing, it will affect everything else around the one sowing that stuff.

Then there's the reality of time and circumstance that simply means that what we visit upon others will eventually be visited upon us. There's also the numbing action that occurs when we act in hateful and deceitful ways—a numbing that robs the robber of the essence of their humanity, therefore robbing them of the whole of life. And finally, in Matthew 16:27, Matthew writes, "For the Son of Man is going to come in his Father's glory with his angels, and then he will reward each person according to what they have done." Justice will be served perfectly.

There are consequences that are tantamount to the destruction of the offender's life. In harming us, they are in turn harming themselves in ways that they cannot imagine, ways that they would likely repent of could they only see it. The perpetrator will eventually be the victim of his own actions. And so, we need to attend to our own pain, but in understanding the horrific loss to our enemy, we can find a place and a space to love them.

CHAPTER 13

Loving Your Enemies: Seeing Ourselves in Our Responses

"Do not judge, and you will not be judged. Do not condemn, and you will not be condemned. Forgive, and you will be forgiven."
—Luke 6:37

"The face of the enemy frightens me only when I see how much it resembles me."

—Unknown Author

WE GET ATTACKED. THAT'S A reality of life. Somewhere, at some time, someone is going to come after us. We've going to be cut or clobbered; we will end up with an assorted collection of contusions. Sometimes the intentions of those who hurt us are misdirected, and at other times, they're completely intentional. Sometimes the actions of others are the stuff of mindless impulse and therefore kind of shotgun in their intention. At other times, the actions of others are completely malicious, being viciously planned and savagely implemented. There are times when the actions of others are based on an errant understanding of events or circumstances, being tragic mistakes and gross misfires. At others times, the intent is simply to hurt us. The nature of the precipitating event is altogether irrelevant, other than being a product of cruelty and by-product of selfishness. When these things happen, we naturally respond. Yet, what does our response say?

WHAT DOES OUR RESPONSE TELL US?

Obviously, we respond. Oddly, our response is often not analyzed because we assume it to be normal or appropriate, given that to which we are responding. If we do, in fact, analyze our response, it's often because we thought that our response was too pensive and tentative, or we thought it was a bit too robust and overwhelming. In other situations, we might think that our response was completely misdirected or somehow inappropriate, given the situation. Then, there are the situations where we feel that we shouldn't have responded at all when we did in fact respond, or we chose *not* to respond when we should have. These kinds of thought processes typically shape any analysis we have about our response.

So, we respond. Whether that response is thought out or thoughtless, we respond. Our focus then tends to be solely on our response, whether it's a good response, a bad response, or a rather irrelevant response. If we swish our response around in the washbasin of our conscience, does it come out looking clean, or is it really dirty? We crunch the facts and massage the feelings as a means of getting a good feel for what we did. We tend to specifically analyze our response instead of analyzing what our response says about us.

There's this crafting, managing, and executing of our response, but nothing about what the response tells us about ourselves. We might be wise to quit looking solely at the response, turn things over, and ask what our response says about us. What does the nature and type and kind of response say about who we are? What does the intensity and direction and flavor of our response suggest about our biases, our beliefs, our personality, our life orientation, our balance or imbalance, or a million other things? Our responses are the fingerprint of our heart and the DNA of our conscience. If we peer into the mirrored reflection of our response, we will see ourselves looking back. Therefore, it might be good to take a good long look in the mirror of our responses, and it might be good to prepare ourselves for a less than savory reflection.

A Bit of Analysis

Fulke Greville wrote that "No man was ever so much deceived by another as by himself." That should create a whole lot of caution within many of us. Of all the people with whom we interact, it is ourselves that we should be analyzing the most. We really can't afford to live our lives walking in introspective darkness as if the darkness is the only thing that we can walk in. We can ill afford to do things like some brainless simpleton, assuming that doing them is just doing them. There's a slothful kind of ignorance that's bred by the fusion of arrogance, narcissism, and a touch of naiveté that results in nothing good. We tend to shy away from introspection, and we briskly engage the world around us without knowing what's going on inside of us. Truth be known, we're much, much more complex than simply a carbon-based mass of mindless responses.

There's a tendency in human behavior to respond without asking why we respond the way we do. Maybe it's something primitive, something that has to do with the whole concept of fight verses flight. When it comes to survival, we don't necessarily have the luxury of stepping back and thoughtfully pondering what we're doing, because we're likely to get eaten alive if we do. Or maybe it's more about convenience, that stopping and thinking and contemplating takes time and energy; maybe in the rush of it all, it's just messy and inconvenient to do that. Or maybe we don't really want to understand why we're doing what we're doing. Maybe that will uncover some less than complimentary things about ourselves that we'd prefer not to know. Or maybe we figure that just feeling the need to do something justifies the doing, so we do it. Yet, we need to know why we do what we do.

WHAT OUR RESPONSES REVEAL:
INSECURITIES

Often, our responses reflect our deep-seated, gnawing insecurities. In some instances, those insecurities result in a response that's wildly disproportionate and entirely over the top. Our insecurities cause us to retaliate in a greater proportion to whatever it was that came at us. In responding like that, we insure that the circumstances or the people who attacked us are sufficiently repelled by us—or better yet, they're outright annihilated. Sometimes an excessive response is the way we get the other person to think twice about messing with us again. At other times, we don't respond at all, fearing that we're likely to incur further attacks or more abuse if we do. So we run and hide. Regardless of the nature of our response, responding out of our insecurities will insure a response that we are certain to regret.

IMMATURITY

Sometimes our responses are entirely misdirected, misallocated, and misapplied; in other words, it's all reflex and no reflection. We haven't quite learned yet that pulling the trigger prematurely may pull disaster right down on our heads. We may not have the maturity to understand fully what happened to us and why it happened. We may not have developed the depth of intellect and insight, and we may not have the balance of maturity in order to render a response that's appropriate to the offense. Or, we may simply take a chainsaw sort of approach, thinking that the nature of the response is irrelevant; we will just have at it rather than taking scalpel in hand and dealing with the situation in a way that's a bit more clean and surgical. So, if our response is rather wild and blithering, we might be immature.

IMPATIENCE

We tend to have a prickly kind of impatience where we find ourselves on pins and needles if things don't roll exactly as we want them to. Impatience means that we want a result right now. Impatience means that we forfeit thinking in favor of doing the deed so that the deed can get done. We forfeit gathering data in favor of dueling it out. We strike out instead of strategizing. We cut people to the quick instead of taking time to contemplate. We retaliate instead of reflect, and we burn hot in the flames of revenge rather than cool our heels in the pool of patience. Our impatience drives us to an immediate, reflexive action that will likely serve to enflame a situation that we're attempting to douse. If our response is knee-jerk, we're likely impatient.

SELFISHNESS

Many times our response is directed to meet our need or serve our agenda. In the fuming mindset of retaliation, we take little if any time to consider the collateral damage of our choices. Collateral damage is a concept that's solely related to the impact that our choices have on others. In most cases, we're not all that much concerned with anybody else. Consequently, the bigger the offense against us, the more we narrow down our response until the focus of our response is nothing more and nothing less than "us" based. If we ignorantly act solely to serve our agenda, we're simply slogging around in the egocentric and brackish backwaters of selfishness. Any response that comes out of that kind of cesspool will be irresponsible. If our actions are all about self-preservation and they spurn the common good, we're selfish. If it's only about us, then it's not about anything good.

MORAL SHALLOWNESS

Most of the time, our responses will challenge our ethics and our morals. When we respond to an attack, the most devastating responses are likely unethical. If we really want to ravage someone and leave the landscape of their lives scorched and barren, that action will probably be immoral or so close to immoral that we'd be stupid to engage it. If we really want to wail on somebody and drive them so far into the ground that they'll never crawl out, we'll probably have to stuff our ethics and live with the guilt of our actions for the rest of our lives. Morality is easily lost in the red-hot heat of hatred and the scorching coals of revenge. If morals aren't guiding our actions, our actions will be misguided.

WHAT OUR RESPONSES SAY ABOUT US

Don't just respond, even though that's the easy thing to do. Ask what your response says about you. Let your responses cause you to respond to you. Ask the hard questions. Do the tough analysis. Face yourself without the nip and tuck of justification, without the Botox of rationalization. You will be a better person who leaves behind a better world even when that world attacks you.

CHAPTER 14

Relationships: Double-Edged

*"As iron sharpens iron, so one person **sharpens** another" [emphasis mine].*

—Proverbs 27:17

"You learn to like someone when you find out what makes them laugh, but you can never truly love someone until you find out what makes them cry."

—Unknown Author

IN THE ODDITY OF A world filled with pain, we are designed for relationship. The oddity of that strange dichotomy rests in the fact that much if not most of the pain that we experience is due to the actions of other people. A staggering amount of our pain emerges from the context of some sort of relationship. Most of our pain is people related, or in some way directly or indirectly caused by the influence of other people. Someone penned that reality quite well when they said that "life would be great if it weren't for people." Yet, while the majority of our pain comes from people, it's relationship that we were designed for.

Take people out of our lives, and our lives might be a bit empty, but we'd likely experience a lot less pain. Without people, our lives would suddenly become less complex and more free. So this thing called "relationship," the very thing that we were intimately designed for and is core to our existence, is the very thing that causes us most of our pain. How it is that what we desperately need is the thing that can be so desperately devastating? What in the world is up with the reality that the very thing that is so absolutely core to our existence is also the thing that can rip us to pieces with such emotionless impunity?

DOUBLE-EDGED

Life is such that the more we need a particular object, a specific goal, a relationship, or whatever it is that we feel we need, the more vulnerable we are to that thing. The greater that something can bless our lives, the greater its ability to be a curse. The more power something has to save us, the more power it possesses to likewise destroy us. In the strange dichotomy of life, things are double-edged, being things that can lavish incredible blessings upon us, while at the same time having inherent within them the power to inflict damage and wreak havoc...sometimes beyond comprehension.

It's interesting that life should have within it such a fragile diversity and such a precarious balance. This diversity renders most of life less than safe and always a risk, possessing a tentative balance that can tip either for us or against us with the slightest wind of happenstance. It all makes life a somewhat perilous journey full of thin and sometimes indefinable lines that we attempt to walk in a manner designed to avoid pain and incur pleasure—if that's remotely possible. We live with an ounce of hope and a pound of fear. Relationships can be a blessing or a curse.

RELATIONSHIPS AS NON-NEGOTIABLE

John Donne penned the famous words, "No man is an island." Living in abject isolation is entirely outside the character and frame of our construct as human beings. We are built for relationship, unfathomably shaped with a hole that only others can fill. If we dare to repel to the innermost, hidden parts of our souls, we will find there a hole of cavernous proportions that only God Himself can fill. Therefore, the need for relationship is not some sort of cute addendum or distantly remote need that all other needs eclipse. Relationships are not a cute sidebar. The need for relationship rests enthroned at our very core, having been implanted as the beating heart of our humanity. From that heart, it pulsates outward in a million different directions, embracing a million different heartbeats.

Antoine de Saint-Exupéry wrote, "Man is a knot into which relationships are tied." Relationship is fundamental to our well-being, a non-negotiable part without which the fullness of our humanity simply can't be experienced. It might even be said that without relationship, the fullness of our humanity itself is called into question. Yet it is here, in this most fundamental place where we are so vulnerable.

THREE INGREDIENTS TO SAFE RELATIONSHIPS

We've lost real relationship because we've abrasively demanded the needs of self. Exercising the needs of self reduces any relationship to that of a tentative acquaintance, sustained on the condition that the individual's needs are met in the exchange. It's all about the take-away and has nothing to do with the investment. Too often, relationship is a calculated encounter of exchange in which the parties position themselves to line the purses of their greed. It's the classic "what's in it for me?" that will ultimately result in nothing for anyone. This is nothing of relationship and nothing of what our deepest needs really are.

First, relationships are mutual interactions that prioritize the other person, putting that individual decisively at the forefront of the relationship. It's selfless. It rests entirely in an investment and has no interest in maneuvering for a pay-off. It's a hallowed, rare, and unique thing where we do something completely unnatural by placing gain aside in favor of giving. It's unnatural but necessary. So to pull it off, we have to be ever vigilant and always diligent, relentlessly referring to the relational compass that maintains true north by asking, "Who am I doing this for?" It's about expenditure of self for the enrichment of another...plain and simple.

Second, the interests of the relationship are placed in a position superior to our own interests. Yet, that relationship is placed second to the interests of the other person. Insuring the sustained strength and ongoing existence of the relationship is primary over securing one's own needs in the relationship. Too often, we see our personal needs as being in competition with the needs of the relationship. Sometimes we fight the relationship in the attempt to get our needs met. The reality is that our core needs are met out of the very bond that's fostered deep in the womb of relationship.

Finally, we ourselves stand third, in a position that is both subordinate and generously life-giving. Relationship by oneself is not relationship; therefore, the position of the individual is of necessity behind that of the other, as well as being behind that of the relationship, which is defined by the sustained union of both parties. We are built up as we bow down. When we liberally pour out, the relationship lavishly pours in. When we give, we are given to. Wearing the lowly robes of servitude ultimately clothes us in the garments of a rich relationship. As James so beautifully puts it, "humble yourselves before the Lord, and he will lift you up" (James 4:10).

Sound Principles Easily Forfeited

Such principles sound reasonable and quite right only because they've been diluted by endless repetition. We've thinned these principles by pouring in cheap talk, but we've never thickened them with sacrificial action. Sure, they're right, but actually doing that which is right distinctly marks the difference between someone who converses and someone who commits. We should be vigilant, realizing that life's greatest truths are often perceived as great and admirable in principle until we are faced with the decision to implement them or not.

Once we're face to face with life's greatest truths, we can finally see how great and admirable they truly are. Once we stand right beside them, we suddenly realize the enormity of their base. Looking up, we try to grasp the dizzying heights to which they tower. Too often, we realize that we prefer to view life's truths from a comfortable distance; our preference is to ponder them from afar. Because that's the case, when we get up close, we tend to decline them and slink away.

Therefore, we have difficulty applying life's truth to relationships. Many so-called relationships look the part. They have some of the characteristics and traits to make them look sufficiently so. The verbiage is good; the interactions at times are intense and at other times joyful. There are rich moments and ones that are likewise meaningful. There is play and prayer, battles and bantering, tender moments and tough trials.

Yet, if the relationship succumbs to the needs of self, it will dissolve into ashes and be scattered to the winds of time and tides of adversity. Two people in a committed relationship who commit themselves to meeting their own needs are committed to the destruction of both the relationship and ultimately themselves.

We would do well to re-evaluate our relationships: friendships, relationships within our families—our spouses and children—and, most importantly, our relationship with God. Do we really have relationships, or do we have a cheap facsimile? Are we walking arm in arm with others, or are we walking with others entirely alone? Is that hole within us achingly empty despite the fact that a crowd is around us? Do we wake up wondering where everyone else is in a world populated with a wide variety of everyone else's? If so, re-evaluate your relationships and the principles upon which you've constructed them. It may transform your life.

Simple Truths for Profound Growth

CHAPTER 15

Our Identity and Value: Internal, Not External

"I want to know Christ—yes, to know the power of his resurrection and participation in his sufferings, becoming like him in his death."
—Philippians 3:10

"When I quit working, I lost all sense of identity in about fifteen minutes."
—Paige Rense

WE NEVER LEARN. OR IF we do, we don't apply the lessons all that well. We're an independent sort, fiercely independent much of the time. Because we are, there's a kind of natural gravitation, an inner pull toward doing things on our own. If we seek help, or too much help, we feel diminished. We tend to bear the brunt, shoulder the load, put our nose to the grindstone, bite the bullet, buck up, suck it up, and go the distance.

Maybe this whole independent mentality has been a product of our life story—having to do it all ourselves because no one was there to help us, or no one did it quite as good or as quickly as we did. Maybe we've been on the receiving end of the gross failures, the idiotic backfires, and reckless misfires of others who constantly let things blow up in our faces. Or maybe there's that need to prove ourselves and to establish our worth. Often we have the need to display our intellectual prowess, to exercise the muscle of our skill set, or flaunt our expertise in order to secure our place in some sort of ill-defined and vague pecking order that defines our sense of worth and value.

In some instances, the striving for independence is directly related to the fact that we've always lived in someone's long shadow and need to show ourselves as bigger than the shadow that was cast upon us—or at least prove that we're as big as the person casting that shadow. At other times, we're out to prove people wrong, to conclusively show beyond any shadow of a doubt that we are competent even though people repeatedly told us otherwise. Typically, it's ourselves that we're really trying to convince; the toughest audience that we play to is ourselves. Then there's the whole thing of "keeping up with the Jones'" that makes it purely a competition for bragging rights. The reasons for these fiercely independent mentalities are many.

THE FATIGUE OF PROVING OURSELVES

The need to prove ourselves is relentless. We typically meet that need through achievement, or at least our attempts at it. We can attempt to pound out or tease out achievements in all kinds of areas in a myriad of ways. It's possible to set a goal for just about anything that we do. Goals give us a readily identifiable marker that lets us define whether we're successful or not. Often our lives are littered with these randomly strewn markers as we set up a criterion for just about everything to the point that just about everything is a defined as a challenge. When it's all a challenge, it's all a competition. And when it's all a competition, our lives become driven to hysteria by the need to win the competition because our identity and value rest in it. The softness of solace, the restorative ointment of reflection, and the untangling moments of uncluttered meandering through life's scarcely trodden paths are lost to souls withering under the scorching demands of competition. In the end, the misguided attempts we've made to prove ourselves leave us with nothing, proving nothing.

THE NEED TO PROVE OURSELVES: IDENTITY AND WORTH

At the core of the need to prove ourselves lies two fundamental needs: first, the need for identity; second, the need for worth and value. Identity and worth are two foundational pillars that are set deep in the bedrock of our hearts and rise into the dizzying stratosphere of our souls. Much of the weight of our lives rests on these pillars. In some lives, these pillars are muscular and firm; in others, they're lean and atrophied, and in some lives, they don't exist at all. Regardless, the strength of our being rests in part on whatever these pillars are or are not.

If the basis of our identity and our sense of worth is rooted in achievement, which is most often defined by the stuff that we do, then we always have to be doing. We have no alternative except to always be on the run, always planning the next thing, and always tediously mapping out the next endeavor to make sure that it's better than the last one. We have to push the envelope, briskly ratchet everything up a notch or two, extend the reach of our grasp, and exhaust ourselves in reaching the peak of our expectations. We're always taking everything we lay our hands on to the next level to the point that we eventually end up putting the next level entirely out of reach.

WHO OR WHAT IS DRIVING US?

William Frederick Book wrote that "a man must drive his energy, not be driven by it." We know that we expend energy, and we typically expend a lot of it. But we rarely question whether we're driving our energy or allowing it to drive us. Who's in control here? We pound, we push, we persevere, and we plod along, and when we are pummeled, we pick ourselves up and press on. The relentless nature rarely if ever gives us the time or the resolve to pull back and ask who's controlling the energy that we're expending. We're expending energy, but are we in control of the expenditure?

If we're not controlling the expenditure of our energy, if we're simply responding or reacting or being driven to circumvent some threat or achieve some lofty goal that we can't in reality achieve, then the energy spent is wasted. The deceptive nature of it all is that, because we're expending energy, we assume we're accomplishing something. It's seems reasonable to assume that a ton of energy expended should equal a ton of accomplishments achieved. The fact that we're doing so much could only result in some sort of goal attainment. Something good and successful must be coming out of this simply because the energy we're putting out has to be resulting in some outcome . . . doesn't it? We might not be able to identify any specific momentum, and the actual achieving of any goals might be vague, but we assume that they're happening because expending that much energy has to bring results.

WHAT DRIVES US DRIVES OUR ENERGY

We've bought into the notion that what we do defines who we are as well as our worth and value. If I don't know who I am, if I don't have any sense of worth or value, my life is irreparably stuck and meaningless. It's a place that none of us can afford to be in because it's a place that we simply can't survive. At our core, we need to know who we are and that we have value. Those two things are simply non-negotiable. So we must have a sense of identity, and we must feel that we possess at least some degree of worth and value. Our natural humanity, as well as the ever-present voice of the culture, constantly screams the tattered mantra that you get all of that stuff through achievement. If that's the case, then I'd better get about the business of achieving.

Because we have embraced this fundamentally frayed line of thinking, our energies become spent on our attempts at achievement.

We've got to achieve. Whether we actually achieve what we're out to achieve neither defines us nor establishes our worth. We might put all that stuff on and masquerade around in a manner that gives us an air of identity and worth, but it's nothing more than air. To figure out who we are, we must put on the shoes of courage and ascend the lofty precipices of our hearts. We have to repel deep within the caverns of our souls. We have to find where we are, and that's typically in the deep places that lay hidden, wildly remote, and often abandoned within us. It's discovering who God masterfully created us to be and understanding that any design of His is always priceless. God's work never needs to be proven. It simply needs to be appreciated. Embracing takes work that's both laborious and frightening. However, that's how we find ourselves. To find ourselves, we go upward in order to go inward so that we can ultimately go outward, not the reverse.

Yet, we default to achievement to do that instead. If we achieve, it all goes away. If we achieve, we can hold up the mirror reflecting what we've achieved, point to it, and say, "see, that's me; that's who I am," when that's not who we are at all. Achievement says we have value because we can point to the contribution of the achievement, that we took "nothing" and made "something" from it, which says that we do have a place and a purpose, when in reality it neither defines nor substantiates either. Our energies are misdirected and wasted because they're controlled, disseminated, and eventually spent out by these illusions.

OUR VALUE IS INTERNAL, NOT EXTERNAL

As insanely mind-boggling as it is, our value rests in who we are, not in what we do with who we are. You may want to read that last line again. What we do is simply a manifestation of who we are. We would be much better served using our energies to bring growth and maturation to who we are, not squandering those energies in our attempts to prove we have value through the veneer of achievement. This is not to say that achievement is bad. In reality, achievement is very good. Rather, achievement for the wrong reasons or misplaced motivations is bad.

Mentally, it's a tough shift to make, but each of us needs to embrace the fact that our value is in who we are. That identity and that value are already there within us, granted and planted from eternity past. Therefore, we don't need to create it or prove it. We only need to rest in it and let everything flow from it. When we do that, achievement becomes fun, exhilarating, and life-changing both for us and all those around us. You have value just because you are who you are. May that be your forever theme.

CHAPTER 16

Releasing Your Grip: Possessing Life Is Letting Life Possess You

"He will no longer be rich and his wealth will not endure, nor will his possessions spread over the land."

—Job 15:29

"To have little is to possess. To have plenty is to be perplexed."

—Lao-tzu

HOLDING ON TO SOMETHING? OF course you are. We all do it. There are things that we feel are of great value. Once we believe that something is of value, we tend to grab onto it. It seems that our one and sometimes only natural reflex is one of possession. We have to have it, so we automatically reach for it.

In reality, we're a fairly insecure bunch. We've pulled off a great mismatch by equating security with possessions. So, insecure as we are, we bolster ourselves with possessions that never create the desired security. But that doesn't give us pause to think about what we're doing. Instead, we keep right on gathering stuff, thinking that when we've got enough of it, we'll be good. With that mentality, we'll be gathering for a lifetime; we'll be gathering nothing but frustration.

The degree to which we grab things and the force of our grip on it are determined by how much we value the object or relationship. If we think a possession or a person can grant us a hefty piece of security, we'll clench it tightly. If it's a conversation piece or an investment that's just a nice addition and firms things up a bit, our grip won't be quite as firm. Because that's the case, our grip can be like a steel trap, or it can be rather loose and supple.

TAKING A LOOK AT OUR GRIP

What's odd is that we don't often think about how tightly we're holding onto certain things. We presume that it's natural and normal to hold onto the things that we value or see as central to our lives or providing that needed security. So we spring the trap, lay out the cash, sign the contract, run the credit card, or use the five-finger discount to get what we want to possess. We falsely assume that once we're in possession of it, we're supposed to always remain in possession of it.

We develop a kind of hoarding management mentality that demands that we hold onto things with a white-knuckled grip so that nothing can peel our fingers off it. The bizarre workings of our minds can go so far as to cause us to hold onto things that don't serve us at all and are simply dead, decaying weight. The fact that we possess things causes us to assume that we're supposed to keep them. What else would we do with them? We assume that holding onto things is natural, necessary, and obviously normal. A blind sense of possession can override a sure-sighted sense of practicality.

WHAT DETERMINES WHAT WE GRAB

So, we inventory what we have in our lives: people, assets, careers, friendships, dreams, goals, relationships, material possessions, various resources. Then we assign each of those things a value based on a grid intricately and tediously constructed from our goals, value systems, present position in life, sense of security or lack thereof, self-esteem, the threats or risks we perceive that we have, or any myriad of determining factors. Our grip on these things is then determined by the value we assess them as having, based on these patchwork grids.

We also inventory what we don't have in our lives but wish to have. We look outside the realm of our possessions to those things that we hope to acquire. Whether those things are fiscal assets, material possessions, various relationships at various levels of relationship, career goals molded by our aspirations, the square footage of our home, the reach of our influence, our place in some social food chain, or the smoothness of the image we want to project to those around us. Whatever we've determined we want will then determine the degree of our grip on the things that it will take to get it. We're all about the business of grabbing people, things, or opportunities to secure our possession of them, or maneuvering ourselves in order to get them.

WHAT ABOUT GRIP?

It's interesting that the harder we hold onto something, the more likely we are to kill it. We assume that strengthening our grip insures the continued possession of the thing or things that we're holding onto. Indeed, our possession is in all probability insured. However, what we don't realize is that we'll possess it all right, but it'll likely be empty and dead. As Pliny the Young aptly put it, "An object in possession seldom retains the same charm that it had in pursuit."

Things that are of real value in life can't be held. The oddity of it all is that the very things we want to possess, the things we expend our lives in some helter-skelter rampage to take hold of, those very things are killed in the possession. That may seem contradictory, but it's true. How many times have we held firmly onto an investment only to lose it despite the iron grip we had on it? In how many instances have we gone to great lengths and dizzying heights to insure the continued possession of a relationship, only to have it slip right through our fingers? How many times have we rigorously secured some sort of asset by nailing it down, fencing it in, sealing it tight, cinching it firmly, locking it down hard, insuring it, putting it in a trust, or somehow solidly encasing it in some tedious manner or fashion only to lose it despite the aggressiveness of our efforts? And in the end, we lose it through death of it.

WHAT DO WE POSSESS?

However, there are times when we feel we haven't lost something despite our grip on it; we're still in possession of it and have it stored away in the vault that we store things away in. We point to those things as evidence that holding onto things doesn't necessarily result in the loss of them. We're confident that we can take hold of things with an iron grip and, despite the iron grip, keep them very much alive.

Yet, can we possess some opportunity or privilege and kill it in the possession? Do the great and wonderful things die if they're held? Is there something about the essential nature of the things that are precious and sacred that in order for them to live, they must be free? Is it possible that captivity is death to stuff of true value? If some glistening object or rare opportunity is truly priceless, then captivity renders it an object that can be possessed. If it can be possessed, then it can be bartered. And if it can be bartered between and among men, is it truly priceless? Possession kills the priceless.

Once it's dead, what is it that we possess? Once the dream is hauled into the boat of our lives as some mammoth catch, does it flounder at the bottom of our boats and then expire in the rancid air of captivity? Once something is netted and caged, the wonder for which it was created is now made entirely irrelevant by the suffocating confines in which we've encased it. We can't put the priceless on display, because the priceless cannot be grasped sufficiently to be put display.

We can hold on to many things and display them to prove that we're still in possession of them while not being in possession of them at all. Things firmly gripped lose their lives and are irrevocably sapped of their vitality. Once depleted, they hold no interest for us anymore, having lost their luster and appeal. Left before us are empty carcasses and hollow shells that have the illusion of being priceless but none of the essence.

POSSESSION IS FOUND IN NOT POSSESSING

If we want to embrace life, we must never set traps for it or cage it. It's in the privilege of observing life in all its unbridled passion and surging forcefulness that we are enriched and satisfied. None of that happens when the priceless is bound by the chains of possession.

Possessing life can only happen in not possessing it. Possessing life is observing it and then romping and frolicking right along with it as a privileged guest. We are honored to be granted the experience. We are bequeathed a great gift in the forever possession of the memory. In reality, we can only possess the experience and the memory if we let life possess us in order to have an experience to remember.

It's giving life permission to have its way with us, not demanding our way with it through the possession of it. Possession of this thing we call life is giving up the possession of ourselves and handing that over to something infinitely bigger than us. It's recognizing that we're on a journey that we didn't create and will only mar and diminish in our attempts to possess it and steer it. Surrendering ourselves and letting ourselves be in the possession of life is the secret to possessing life.

So, what are you holding onto? People? Possessions? Time? An investment? A dream? A relationship? Maintaining your physical attractiveness? Whatever it is, it's going to die. Maybe you need to free yourself to be in the possession of something greater than you and realize that everything that you've looked to have in the mad race of possession is right there within you. Free yourself to have the experience without the encumbrances of having to own it. It's amazing how we are released when we release our grip.

CHAPTER 17

Success: Defining It Defines Us

"Truly I tell you, anyone who will not receive the kingdom of God like a little child will never enter it."

—Luke 18:17

"Nothing succeeds like the appearance of success."

—Christopher Lasch

ALL OF US WANT SUCCESS. We're not stagnant creatures just milling about and burning time until we drop dead. There's something more intentional about us, a compelling predisposition to respond to challenges, and a natural inclination to set goals, whether we actually achieve them or not. We have a need to have a purpose, a defining rationale that identifies us as more than carbon-based life forms going through a series of meaningless motions on our meandering way to the grave. We have a need to achieve, to conquer, to rise to great heights and soar. It seems that being alive is not enough to justify our existence or lend value to that existence. Rather, we have to make our mark and leave a legacy that shouts that we were more than people who simply lived out our days.

This need to justify our existence naturally comes in the desire to succeed in some way. Success seems to justify our existence. The need to succeed speaks to the fact that we're made to achieve things. It's in us to create, and to create successfully. Our problem is that this need has long overstepped its bounds as we've given it permission to define our worth. Success appears to give our existence some kind of tangible credibility that's convincing enough for us to believe that we're worth the space that we take up. It sells us on ourselves, at least enough to believe that we're worth having around, if nothing else.

How We Define Success

To know if we have value, we have to define success. How do we know if we've succeeded if we don't have some sort of standard by which to define it? What will give us a sense that we've accomplished something, whatever that might be? How will we determine how far we've come or how far we've yet to go? Did we do it right, or did we do it wrong? Did what we do have value, or were we just showboating, strutting around the stage of our lives and doing a cute but classless song and dance? Have I made the grade, done the deal, cut the mustard, and gone the whole nine yards? To answer those questions, we have to define what the grade is, what the deal looks like, how cut mustard's supposed to look, and how far nine yards really is. In other words, we have to define success. Otherwise, we have no yardstick that we can use in order to determine our progress or lack thereof.

The Difficulty in the Definition

The problem for most of us is not in succeeding. The real issue is in how we define success. Until we define it, we won't know if we've achieved it. Whatever our definition turns out to be, it's extremely powerful. Our definition of success has influence beyond our recognition. That definition has implications for us that never even dawn on us. How we define success will determine what we do and how we do it. Success as we define it becomes the compass that locks us onto a specific course that's precisely pointed toward whatever we've defined success as being. Our definition of success will quite literally direct the whole of our energies; it will channel the vast expanse of our experiences and herd the accumulated assets of all of our resources toward that definition.

Our definition of success will determine what risks we take, exactly what we're willing to sacrifice, what we'll lay on the chopping block, how many hits we're willing to take, how far we're willing to fall, and to what lengths we'll be willing to go. In the end, it will be the very thing that determines the degree to which we've achieved or failed. Our definition of success becomes the yardstick by which we measure both what we do and ultimately what we're worth. It can become the idol at whose feet we bow and to which the whole of our lives and our energies are sacrificially expended. It can become the focal point of what we do. Therefore, our definition of success becomes terribly critical.

OUR DEFINITION DEFINES OUR VALUE

Our definition of success is driven by whatever our ultimate goal is. There are tons of goals that we could sort and sift through, discuss, evaluate, and weigh. However, at the core of each goal, there's typically one central goal that defines all other goals. That fundamental goal is to have a sense that our lives have "value." Whatever our goals are and whatever they look like, it's likely that their main objective and core purpose is to convince ourselves that we have value. Our having value justifies our existence and validates that we're worthy of the air we breathe and the food that we eat. Having a sense of value is core to our humanity because without it we feel empty, hollow, entirely lost, and totally unworthy. Despite how remarkably gifted or talented we might be, without a sense of value, it all comes to naught. Value is indispensable.

The way that we convince ourselves that we have value is by convincing others that we have value. It's a kind of self-inflicted sales job, where we get others to believe that we have value, which in turn convinces us that we have value. Until others see it in us, we can't possibly believe that we have it. Others become a mirror in whose surface we must see broad smiles, heads nodding in approval, and affirming gestures that communicate to us in their reflections that we have value.

Because that's frequently the case, as sad as that might be, our definition of success is built on and around doing something that others will look at in awe or reverence, be driven to emulate, hold in high esteem, or find praiseworthy because it's so mesmerizing and grand. Whatever we do, it has to be spectacular, ingenious, creative, innovative, and daring. It must be generously packed with all the other electrifying adjectives that lend it grandness and ascribe it value. Once others grant our efforts value, we grant them value. When we grant them value, we grant ourselves value because now we've got proof that we have value. And so, our definition of success has to continuously generate outcomes that people will value so that we can stuff ourselves full of that "stuff" sufficiently enough to feel that we have value.

A Better Definition – What It Is and What It Isn't

A definition of success is not so much about success as it is about standards. It's not about accolades as much as it's about authenticity. It's not about strategy; it's about sanctity. It's not about where one wants to go; it's about living well right where we are. It's not about what one does, but who one is. Success is based on how we choose to live, which dictates what we choose to do, not the other way around. Success is the maintenance of virtue and the life-long refining of a right heart when the world around us sees no value in either of these—or anything else admirable, for that matter. Success is a commitment to an unwavering morality for the sole purpose of morality and not for any applause that such a stance might obtain for us. Success is not in what we do, but how we did it.

Albert Einstein put it this way when he said, "Try not to become a man of success, but rather try to become a man of value." Success is living well and dying with that legacy left in our wake. It's not about how many people witnessed our living well or how many can attest to it at the end. It's simply that we were those things, whether they were displayed in front of masses of people or lived out in the greater testing ground of total isolation where no one sees but God. Success is a life well lived, regardless of how many trophies, certificates, promotions, or contracts we got in the process of living. The marks of real success can't be hung on a wall, deposited in a bank account, or used as leverage to advance a career. Success is not found in the size of the trusts we leave behind or in the lofty phrases carved in granite epitaphs on our tombstones. Those things are more the stuff of achievement, which are good, but they're not necessarily "success."

It's not that achievements, or diligently working for success, are bad. They're not. It's simply that they're not the hallmark of the kind of success that shapes lives, transforms people, rocks cultures, calls others to higher ground, and boldly exhibits something far beyond the tiny confines of our human existence and something more of the massive character and essence of the God who created us. Success is right living, exuberantly virtuous living, mindful living, and selfless living that combine to result in a bold living that can be stunning. It's all lived out without wondering how many brownie points we're going to amass by living that way and how good it's all going to look to everyone around us. It's not about calculating how many cheers we can generate to raise the roof or how many "Atta boys" we can accumulate in order to fill some dry ocean of admiration. It's just living with integrity for the sake of living that way and nothing more. That's success.

An Adjustment

Our culture ties success to achievement as defined as worthy and worthwhile in and by our culture. Yet, real success is a life well lived regardless of the achievements or lack thereof. Live right. Live well. Live with integrity. Be guided by a strong morality. Be a stand-up person in a world that's too often standing down. Be fearless in your faith and immovable in your morality. Stun others by letting them see actions, choices, and behaviors that are inherently good in ways they've never seen in themselves. Stand for all that's good and right even when the world around you is falling for all that's bad and wrong. That's success. That's worth living for and dying in. Re-define success for yourself and then live it brazenly.

CHAPTER 18

Taking Ourselves Too Seriously: The Weight that We Carry

"Pride goes before destruction, a haughty spirit before a fall."
—Proverbs 16:8

"An expert is one who knows more and more about less and less until he knows absolutely everything about nothing."
—Author Unknown

WE LIVE WITH OURSELVES 24/7. Every morning we get up with ourselves, we walk through our days with ourselves, we wrestle with ourselves, we ponder ourselves, we get angry at ourselves, we question ourselves, we love and hate ourselves in a curious sort of emotional dance, and at the end of the day, it's ourselves who we crawl into bed with. We're thoroughly embedded in our heads and no one else's, even though we may try to find a way to finagle ourselves into at least a couple of the heads around us. When we look in the mirror, we see ourselves looking back—typically with a slight sigh of monotonous repetition. Yeah, we live in us and with us.

We live in the world of our own opinions, life experiences, abilities, and senses. We're in the company of our own company even when we'd sometimes prefer to take a break from our own company. We can't take a break from ourselves even when we'd like to break off our own relationship with ourselves for a bit. So, we're immersed with ourselves because we're always in the company of ourselves and enmeshed in a world largely defined by ourselves.

Because we're in our own company all the time, we often take ourselves far too seriously. Certainly, there are times when we don't take ourselves seriously enough. There are times when we spend a lot more time diminishing ourselves than is good for us. But if we tend to err on one side or the other, we'd probably have to admit that we often think too much of ourselves, and we function out of that perception.

THE WORLD PROMPTS THE SELF

The world we live in seems to have a hand in perpetuating that mentality as well. The world we live in can be a threatening place. Danger lurks in many different places wearing many different disguises with many different agendas. Because that's the world we have to navigate day in and day out, we naturally tend to adopt a stance of self-preservation. Given the unfortunate reality that many people are out for themselves, it doesn't take us long to realize that if we're not looking out for our own selves, someone will take advantage of us in the process of looking out for themselves. So we hunker down, pull ourselves into ourselves, throw up a myriad of complex defense mechanisms, pledge allegiance to our agendas, and cautiously press on.

GETTING IT DONE PROMPTS THE SELF

We've also found out that if we don't do things ourselves, it's unlikely that someone else is going to do them for us. The whole "get 'er done" attitude is based on us getting it done, not someone else because that "someone else" probably won't show up. If perchance they do, they're "gonna get 'er done" all right, but they're probably going to "get it done" for themselves. Who's going to do it for us if we don't? It doesn't take much concentrated brain power to figure out that nothing's going to be handed to us; people aren't going to spend their lives spending their energies on us. So, in most cases, we must rely on ourselves.

THE CULTURE PROMPTS THE SELF

While it's a bit dulling and redundant, the cultural mentality tends to lean toward a mentality of self. It sounds rather distasteful, and I doubt that any of us really wants to hear it. However, we live in a culture that elevates the self. We all like to talk about the good of the common man. The whole "we're our brother's keeper" thing is ethically robust. But when it all caves in and we're facing a challenge that's potentially threatening, the good of the common man is typically the good of "this man," meaning us. Stewardship and charity are immensely life enriching. Yet, too frequently, we place ourselves on the receiving end of those endeavors so that we're our own charitable organization. That whole mentality of these types of behaviors is repeatedly reinforced because the culture rewards those who reward themselves.

DECEPTIVE AGENDAS

Many of us figure that if we get ourselves situated (whatever that looks like), then we'll have the resources to reach out to others. We incessantly fill the storehouses of our aspirations, thinking that once we've filled them, we'll generously spoon off the sweet excesses and munificently pour that out into the lives of others. With that mentality undergirding our actions, we collect and hoard and purchase and barter, relieved of any sense of materialism or guilt, believing that—in the end—it's really about everyone else.

The problem with that is knowing what "situated" looks like. When is enough, enough? When are we positioned sufficiently to spoon off those sweet excesses and really reach out to others? At what point do we have enough money, enough resources, enough stock options, enough experiences, a network that's broad enough, sufficient time, ample energy, and adequate internal fortitude to reach out to others? When is it all big enough so that skimming a little off the top won't jeopardize anything else? When is "enough" sufficient enough to sustain itself at the point we start distributing those sweet excesses?

Two things tend to happen in this scenario. The first is that the more we get "situated," the more we want to get more "situated." There's a tendency to want things to be just a touch more solid. We want to make things just a little bit firmer. We want to add just one more layer to the foundation. General Douglas MacArthur said, "There is no security on this earth; there is only opportunity." It's part of our fearful nature to work to generate more security, and in doing that, we miss opportunity.

The second problem is that the more we get "situated," the more comfortable we tend to become. The more comfortable we become, the less motivated we are to reach out to others because it's just too exhausting to leave the armchair of comforts we've amassed. We play armchair quarterback with charitable thoughts that never leave the comfort of our armchairs. So, we settle down and ponder our stuff, forgetting the people.

THE ALTERNATIVE

It seems that if we're going to take ourselves too seriously, we should do so in relation to other people. If we want to take ourselves seriously, we should do so in direct correlation with how seriously we take others. If our investment is primarily in others, we should take ourselves seriously in that endeavor. Our value then is not fundamentally inherent in us and all the things that we've amassed, but in the way the things we have amassed can serve others. Our value rests in what we can expend in the service of others and not in the service of self.

That posture mercifully and abruptly shifts the focus away from us. Our value rests in an investment, not in an emotional incest where we're captivated with ourselves for the sake of ourselves and out of the love that we have for ourselves. Rather, we take ourselves seriously because it's about people other than us.

We are not here for ourselves, despite a culture that pounds that mandate into frail and eager minds. The fact that we're not here for ourselves is evident in the lives of those who have decided to be here for themselves. Those who live for themselves deteriorate and wane in the terminal cancer of selfishness. Feeding self is nothing more than starving self in a slow suicide. We gorge our assets plump and rotund, while we starve our hearts and famish our souls.

There is no energy in the service of self, but there is abundant energy in the service of others. There is no refreshment in feeding the cravings of self, but there is lavish refreshment nurturing the starving people that lie all around us. There's no abiding satisfaction in gorging the lusts of self, but there's a rich cornucopia of life-long blessings in lifting up the fellow man. If it's directed to us, it might be sweet and succulent for a moment, but it will quickly become bitter and gristle-like in our mouths. If it's directed to others, it will be sweet and succulent in ways we could have never imagined, and it will feed us always.

TAKING YOURSELF TOO SERIOUSLY

If there's a certain deathblow that will knock us flat and leave us for dead, it's taking ourselves too seriously. Take yourself seriously by taking others seriously. Get away from the mirror and instead see yourself reflected in the eyes and heart of another. Live not for self, for in doing so you live to the death of self. Don't take yourself too seriously, or you will take yourself to the death of yourself.

CHAPTER 19

The Bottom Line: What Drives Our Decisions

"I was enraged by their sinful greed; I punished them, and hid my face in anger, yet they kept on in their willful ways."

—Isaiah 57:17

"Our choices add up; each one influences others, and cumulatively a series of delightful short-term choices can leave us much worse off in the long run."

—Daniel Akst

WE MAKE DECISIONS ALL DAY, every day, whether those decisions are the redundant routine things that fill up most of our days or the seminal moments that alter our lives for the rest of our lives. Some of the decisions we make are conscious choices that are the product of much time, rigorous thought, the balancing out of potential consequences, weighing the pros and cons, performing analysis to the point of paralysis, and drawing on whatever our resources might be to make the best possible decision. Our decisions may be well researched, talked about, prayed about, stewed over, mulled over, poured over, and turned over in our heads until our heads hurt.

At other times, our decisions are entirely unconscious, being more reflexive, habitual, and instinctual. Sometimes those decisions are made on the run, navigating whatever's coming at us. Often we don't have the time to think, and we have no space to ponder what needs pondering. The minute that we might use to think about our decision is already packed with other agendas and demands that are already more than what those sixty seconds can hold. On top of that, the next thing in our lives is already upon us, having shown up too early—like some uninvited relative. Hot on its heels, the thing after that is already well on its way to our front door with whatever demands it's going to make on us. So, we make decisions in a reflexive, unconscious kind of way because that's all we can do.

DECISION BEING A CHOICE

Decisions occur when we make a choice. A choice implies that we have options, that we have an array of possibilities, directions, or resources to choose from. Without options, we don't have a choice, for there is no other choice to make. Therefore, the existence of a choice likewise indicates the existence of options.

The process of making a choice often involves narrowing down those options in order to embrace a single option. That involves the insightful processes of inductive and deductive thinking. It thoroughly embraces and intimately engages the exercise of knowledge, wisdom, and discernment in order to select the best option of the many options that might present themselves to us. It's a process of elimination where all the options but one have been discarded in either a rather contemplative, studious manner or a careless thought process that resembled a chaotic flight to somewhere other than here.

The other approach is that we do a bit of picking and choosing, blending several possible options, or parts of options, into a single, workable option. Sometimes the best choice is a shrewdly merged compilation of several choices. It might be likened to baking a cake where the end product is a careful amalgamation of numerous ingredients and not the product of just one ingredient. Being freed from the cramping confines of a single choice to the exponentially expanded possibilities of several choices can be exhilarating.

However we go about it, we spend our lives making choices that are the shifting through of options. Yet, what causes us to ultimately land upon a final choice?

What Drives Our Decisions?

What drives our decisions, whether those decisions are conscious or unconscious? What's the underlying stuff that shapes, chauffeurs, channels and directs the choices we make? We can naively assume that our choices are based solely on our options. We can presume that what drives our choices depends on what we have to choose from at the time we have to make the choice. We can believe that the limitations that we have at the time we're making the choice, as well as the practical implications of the choice—both long-term and short-term—is what really causes us to decide whatever it is that we decide. In other words, we tend to assume that what dictates our choice is whatever's going on as we make it.

It seems that the real truth of the matter is that the things that drive our decisions are much less about the reality of those decisions, and much more about our underlying value system. What drives our decisions is a developed belief system that's much more core to who we are. The chemistry and alchemy of our decisions arises from core values that shape our perception and our thinking. To say that our choices are nothing more than a mix of all the stuff that our present options represent cheapens the ability we have as humans to make powerful decisions in the most difficult of situations. We're driven less by the realities of what we're facing and more by the core values, beliefs, and ethics that lay deep within us. We're not simply aboriginal, carbon-based life forms responding to some sort of primitive chemical reaction to the actions and reactions of the world around us. That rather gullible orientation renders us little more than thinly skin-covered biological androids functioning out of some lengthy series of robotic calculations. We are more than that.

There are fundamental core values that we might not recognize at all, that we might not be able to articulate, and that we might deny wholeheartedly. We have core values that we've intentionally developed, and we have other core values whose origins are entirely unknown. We are driven by deep passion, core convictions, bedrock values, staunchly held beliefs, profound histories, unfathomable emotions, unassailable cognitive processes, and deeply engrained opinions. The depth of these and their centrality in our lives is such that they affect all that we do, whether we realize that or not.

Exactly What Are Our Values?

What kind of core values do we possess? What do our values look like? Exactly what are the values that we hold to? What's the nature of them? What exactly do we believe, anyway? The holding of core values does not mean that those values are sound, right, moral, ethical, or anything else, for that matter. Core values can be rotten to the core. So, presuming that we have values doesn't mean that we have good values. Yet, good or bad, we all have core values.

In making decisions, we need to understand that those decisions will be a direct reflection of our core values, whether those values are positive or negative, healthy or unhealthy, ethical or immoral, selfish or selfless, shallow or deep. Our decisions are a concise and tightly focused mirror of our values. That mirror can be crystal clear or entirely smudged. Either way, it's a reflection of what we hold deep within ourselves.

We then need to realize that our choices are not wholly based on the reality of the options presented to us or the dynamics that we're dealing with. Our decisions are not wholly the carefully crafted outcomes of carefully weighed facts and carefully considered repercussions. The weight of our underlying value system will always be far heavier than the realities of the options before us and the reality of the dynamics that surround those options. More than anything, our choices are a product of our core values and less a product of our acumen. Whether slight or significant, our core values will tip the scale in their direction. That's the power of them.

A LOOK AT OURSELVES

An unknown author wrote, "When one bases his life on principle, ninety-nine percent of his decisions are already made." Our core values decide our decisions. We would do well to take a very long and careful look at our decisions—they are a direct reflection of the core values that we hold. Our decisions may reflect values that are sound, balanced, ethical, moral, and resonating with sustaining depth. On the other hand, our decisions may reflect values that are selfish, unethical, imbalanced, and lacking of any real substance to render them timeless or timely. Either way, our true reflection is revealed in the mirror of our choices and decisions.

So, as you peer into this mirror, what do you see? You may not like what you see, but look into it anyway and decide what, if anything, you want to do with the reflection that stares back at you. If you don't like it, change it. If you happen to like what you see, you may want to ask how to keep that reflection solid and vibrant and how to further build on it and enhance it. Regardless, your choices and your decisions reflect who you are at your core. It's all worth a good look, and it's worth some serious reflection.

Chapter 20

The Worst Slavery: Slavery to Ignorance

"Then Moses said to the people, 'Commemorate this day, the day you came out of Egypt, out of the land of slavery, because the LORD brought you out of it with a mighty hand.'"

—Exodus 13:3

"For some slaves, the first step out of bondage is to learn to see their lives with new eyes. Their reality is a social world where they have their place and some assurance of a subsistence diet. Born into slavery, they cannot easily re-define their lives outside the frame of enslavement."

—Kevin Bales

SLAVERY AS AN INSTITUTION IS pretty far removed from the minds of most of us residing here in twenty-first century America. Slavery sits back far enough in the faded, brittle pages of history to create a more than comfortable chasm between us and itself. We view that chasm of time, social development, and modernism as broad enough to keep slavery from leaping from the past across the chasm of time into the present. The idea of slavery seems to evoke dusty black and white tintype images of the Civil War, the expansive plantations of the Deep South, bloodied chains, inhuman whippings, lynchings, and wild-eyed slaves fleeing through swamps, thick underbrush, and the wilderness of their own fear.

Those kinds of pictures have become our definition of slavery, the visual that creates a picture of what slavery is. Slavery is seen as a physical captivity that coerces a forced service to an enslaving master. That definition is nearly exclusive, making our definition of slavery so incredibly tight that we can't see any other kind of slavery at all. And if we don't see slavery of this type, we assume freedom. That assumption in and of itself can be enslaving.

SLAVERY TO IGNORANCE

Martin Luther King, Jr. wrote, "Nothing in all the world is more dangerous than sincere ignorance and conscientious stupidity." Ignorance is being oblivious, to one degree or another, to the obvious. Confucius said that "ignorance is the night of the mind, but a night without moon and star." Ignorance is walking around in the dark without realizing what dark is, and having no understanding of light.

It's not seeing what actually *is* to the point that whatever it is that *is*, isn't...at all. It's having no recognition of some *thing* that exists, despite how very real and very powerful that thing might be. Ignorance is naiveté multiplied to blindness. It seems that living in blindness can be freeing in some cases, but horrifically dangerous in others.

The old adage that "ignorance is bliss" is blissfully ignorant of how much damage we can experience walking in that kind of darkness. Despite all of that, the worst kind of ignorance is when we're ignorant of being ignorant. It's one thing to intentionally ignore what's in front of us, behind us, or coming at us and turn a blind eye to it. It's quite another thing to be so ignorant that we don't even know that anything is there to turn a blind eye to. Ignorance at its fullest is fully convincing. It sells us wholesale on the hypnotically appealing belief that there's nothing to be ignorant about because there's nothing out there *to* be ignorant about. We buy the bill of goods because it's what we want to believe, regardless of whether it's really believable or not. At that point, slavery leaps out of tintypes and right into our worlds.

Ignorance can open the doors to a lot of things and give a whole lot of space for a whole lot of things to exist in our lives. Yet I think that ignorance of our enslavement is one of the worst types of all of the kinds of slavery to which we can be shackled. We become ignorant to slavery and slaves to ignorance, and we don't even know it.

What Enslaves Us?

How many things enslave us? We tend to see that things make demands of us, that we struggle with certain behaviors or attitudes, that we have our holes to pull ourselves out of, and our mountains to climb over. We look at our lives and see what we need to change, what should be altered, where we need the proverbial "nip n' tuck," a bit of "cut and paste," or maybe a little bit of Botox for the personality. We likewise see the pieces of ourselves that need to be eliminated in some sort of wholesale, demolition-like fashion.

We see our foibles, the fallacies of false fronts, our warts, and other areas that warrant our attention. We know that we're not where we should be and that where we should be isn't anywhere along the road we've been traveling. We know at times that our values have been compromised, our integrity has been marred, and that far too often our morality has had the oxygen completely sucked out of it. We realize that we've crafted career strategies that have outright killed our marriages, that we've sacrificed families to seize six figure incomes. We know that we haven't been accountable when we should have been, we haven't apologized when we should have, and we've not restored even half of what we've stolen along the road of our lives. We know.

IGNORANCE IN ACTION

Yet, we tuck these things in the deep file of ignorance, and then we file it away in the cabinet of forgetfulness. Once we do that, we make every effort never to pull the file again. Yet, nothing is filed, and no filing cabinet exists, despite the ingeniously creative wealth of our imaginations to make it so. In reality, we walk with all of this stuff hanging on with claws embedded in our hearts and roots thickly entwining our souls. Yet, we ignore this. We skip and cavort through life to some sort of fabricated tune whose velvety verses sooth us with lyrics that assure us all is good and our lives are squeaky clean and polished to a mirrored surface.

Or, we manipulate ourselves into believing that the good that we have is good enough—that life is more about the business of survival, which doesn't afford us the larger luxury of introspection, personal evaluation, and the sweaty rigor of change. We don't see anyone else focusing on all that negative stuff, and so we assume that it must not be all that bad, or everyone else would be focusing on it…wouldn't they? We find some comfort in the belief that, overall, we're good people, and at least we *try* to do the good thing, even if we don't end up doing the good thing.

We create expansive and ornate rationalizations to justify ignorance, and we do a bang-up job of creating them. Once we create them, we nail them to the walls of our conscience so that we have them for ready reference during the times when guilt handily rankles our souls. We lull ourselves into the belief that, in the end, all of that stuff really doesn't matter all that much anyway and that it will sort of eventually fall off behind us and kind of blow off the road of our lives, somehow getting lost somewhere in the wilderness of our journey. Therefore, we settle in ignorance and let ignorance give all these things space to enslave us.

OUR ENSLAVEMENT

We are a peculiar people indeed. We tend to focus on the tasks that will either achieve our goals or keep our heads above water, whatever our situation might be. We're notorious for feeding, watering, and carefully attending to all the superficial stuff, but we put the real stuff out of sight behind the veil of ignorance. And we live as slaves to that stuff.

We work to tactfully (or not so tactfully) counter the real stuff, and we futilely attempt to offset it by managing and manipulating the superficial things and focusing on the things that don't hit us too hard or upset us too much. Yet all of our efforts to offset all of the things stored deep in catacombs of ignorance are wholly insufficient. We live trying to change things by ignoring them. We attempt to resolve them by countering them with some other action or direction that isn't as difficult or problematic to deal with. Or we justify them with conveniently trite sayings or offbeat philosophies that act like cooling waters on the searing hot coals of our conscience. In all of this maneuvering, we try to cheat ourselves to health and wholeness.

The end result is slavery to those things we've chosen to ignore. They drive us to futility, attempting to compensate for them by ignoring them. They pound and thunder and bend us from behind the veil of ignorance. They dog our steps and flog our minds. They draw us down and drag us out. They impale us as they impact us. In short, we become subject to them whether we wish to acknowledge it's happening or not. We become so enslaved by our own foolish and shortsighted vision that we become ignorant to that which enslaves us. When that happens, we become slaves in the most awful manner possible.

REFUTE AND REFUSE IGNORANCE

We refute and refuse ignorance by being honest about our weaknesses and failures. We need to cast off justification and torch rationalization. We need to frankly acknowledge and bring to the forefront all of those things in our lives that we've chosen to ignore. Once we do that, we work through them with diligence and beat them by resolving them. In that way, our enslavement can truly end because that which enslaved us is that which we've enslaved through its elimination.

CHAPTER 21

Uniqueness: Looking Beyond Labels to See Strengths

"For you created my inmost being; you knit me together in my mother's womb. I praise you because I am fearfully and wonderfully made; your works are wonderful, I know that full well."

—Psalm 139:13-14

"Today you are You, that is truer than true. There is no one alive who is Youer than You."

—Dr. Seuss

DID YOU EVER NOTICE THAT we seem to be on a relentless quest? That we're scrutinizing ourselves raw in order to ascertain what we think our flaws, foibles, weaknesses and warts are? We put ourselves under a dissecting microscope with skewed lenses in order to ferret out all of our little imperfections. We crawl around on all fours with our eyes mere centimeters from the surface of our lives, scratching and picking and sorting so that everything that we are is entirely clean, socially acceptable, without cultural blemish, and perfectly in step with the people or circumstances or beliefs that we've chosen to determine our steps. With our noses to the ground on an outrageously mad hunt for any and all imperfections, we whittle away our lives being what we think we're supposed to be rather than being who we were created and designed to be. Ever notice?

Ever notice that this incessantly mad hunt never stops? As it is transpiring, it's always rolling right along. Things that never stop typically don't because they weren't designed with a finish in mind. They're perpetual because they can't be accomplished. The only thing that can be accomplished is the pursuit of them. And so we pursue the ferreting out of blemishes and the acquisition of blessings with no goal in mind other than the pursuit of a goal that will never be anything more than a pursuit.

WHAT SETS THE STANDARD FOR OUR SEARCH?

There's certainly a standard in our culture. There are expectations that clearly outline who and what we're supposed to be. There's a variety of scrupulously crafted social templates that we're supposed to ram and cram ourselves into. We have an ever-evolving hodge-podge of plug-and-play scripts that we're expected to memorize and then recite in suave and silky intonations. All of these social expectations are based on culturally acceptable norms that create "cookie-cutter" stereotypes. Stereotypes perpetuate the cultural norms by preserving themselves in the confining formaldehyde of bias so that they can be extracted and applied in all places.

An unknown author wrote, "Stereotypes are devices for saving a biased person the trouble of learning." The worst bias that we can have is a bias about ourselves, as it saves us the trouble of learning that we're a whole lot more than we thought ourselves to be. A bias also saves an incessantly busy culture the time of really looking deeply into itself in order to ascertain the wealth within it. And so we press and contort ourselves in order to fit into the specimen container a cultural stereotype has designed and we listlessly succumb to the formaldehyde.

ONE SIZE FITS ALL

Society too often creates a "one size fits all" kind of mentality. The assumption is that there are slots to fill and we must fill the slots. Find your place, get in it, and stay there. Figure out the cadence and march accordingly. Find your box, move in, decorate it, set up shop, and be happy. What color is your parachute, what's your social standing, what's your breeding and background, what's your disposition, what's your passion, what's your career, and how's your personality wired? Once you've figured all that out, set it aside, take a number, get in line, and realize you're just one of the crowd.

In many cases, the standards of society are good, meaningful, and productive. There are a large number of societal standards that are worthy of our emulation. However, society too often sets standards for society, not the individual. Society often wants it clean, uncomplicated, tight, and easy, so just find your place in line and get in. Because that's often the mindset, cultural expectations are designed to fulfill and achieve that mindset. In succumbing to it, we lose our individuality, we sacrifice the resources of that individuality, and we slowly morph into the indistinguishable blob of the culture.

DISCOVERING OUR UNIQUENESS

The balance that few people seem to achieve is one where we purposefully cultivate the core of who we are while working to slough off the biasing sludge that the culture seems to spill on us. It's getting down to who I am, but not as part of the sludge-like cultural stew. Instead, it's identifying who I am as a uniquely separate ingredient that smells sweet and potent when it stands alone, and adds a one-of-a-kind flavor to the stew when a pinch of it is added to the mix.

It's not about a blatant disregard for cultural norms or expectations at all. Rather, it's being committed to our uniqueness as a person rather than being rigorously force fit into a mold of the culture's choosing. It's realizing that when we maximize who we are, we are then of maximum benefit to society and the world around us. Our individuality is an asset to our culture. Yet, before we can be authentically "us," we must determine who or what that "us" is. In more effectively making that determination, there are a few thoughts you might want to start with:

UNDERSTANDING OUR LIMITATIONS

First, healthy self-evaluation takes place when we're honest about our limitations. Sometimes our limits should be exactly that: our limits. Wisdom often involves knowing when to stop, when far enough is far enough, and when it's legitimately time to invest our energies elsewhere. Limitations exist for reasons. It's not about giving up, surrendering, being weak-willed, or passively apathetic. It has nothing to do with being sheepish, shy, insecure, or outright scared. Rather, limitations let us know when some task is completed, that further work on our part is unnecessary, that anything beyond this point is squandered energy, and that we need to direct our resources toward the next place in our lives. Limits let us know that sometimes things can be ruined through excess and that we all reach times and places where stepping away is the final touch.

DEVELOPING REALISTIC EXPECTATIONS

Second, effective self-evaluation takes place when we're realistic about our expectations. Our expectations can be too high, too low, entirely misdirected, or so vague that we couldn't even tell someone what they were. Expectations define what we expect of ourselves, and they typically say volumes about how we feel about ourselves. Lack of expectations either suggests a sloth-like laziness, a blatant ignorance about life, a disregard for the gift of life and the single shot we have at it, or a glaring lack of self-confidence. Realistic expectations cannot be the stuff of wildly irresponsible ideas or the product of fear-based barriers. They should reflect the genuine capabilities of our uniqueness that will create the most balanced environment within which our uniqueness can flourish. Accurate expectations allow us to avoid living with the perilous lie that we're somehow more than what we really are. More profoundly, they give us permission to be fully ourselves while forbidding that we be anything less.

SELF-EVALUATION OUTSIDE OF OUR VISION

Third, healthy self-evaluation occurs when we view ourselves through the template of a belief system that calls us out, up, and beyond our own humanity to believe in our ability to embrace a design that's infinitely higher and more profound than the lax designs of a mediocre culture. It's believing that the vision of who we can be is dramatically limited by *our* vision of who we can be. It's believing that something greater than us has something much greater in mind for us. If we're not careful, we forfeit vision for confining rubrics because they seem more reasonable and much more doable. We then embrace a pathetic and unnecessary compromise that spreads the aggressively infesting germ of mediocrity throughout our lives. We can eradicate the germ of mediocrity by looking back at ourselves through the eyes of an entity much bigger than us who sees us as big as we really are.

WE ARE MORE

Few of us do any kind of self-evaluation with anything remotely resembling the kind of depth that unleashes us. We gullibly embrace the lax and plastic cultural expectations. We're diminished by our own assessment of ourselves, an assessment that wholly abandons our uniqueness. We rarely embrace a framework that even comes close to allowing us to see the immensity of who we are, that based on that understanding beckons us to be humbled in the stunning recognition of who we are, and that challenges us to draw upon the resources around us to build upon the immense resources within us. We are more than we presume ourselves to be—much, much more.

That realization is liberating and terrifying all at once. By grasping it, the ponderous shackles of stereotypes fall at our feet, freeing us as never before. Yet, freedom means responsibility and risk. And that may be too much. Yet, whatever the "more" is that we are, it's completely sufficient for a life of "more." We can rest in the fact that we are enough. In fact, with God we are more than the obstacles, challenges, and risks that stand before us, around us, above us, below us, and beyond us. Look beyond the labels and see your strengths.

CHAPTER 22

Uniqueness: Uniqueness Not as License

"Eli's sons were scoundrels; they had no regard for the Lord."
—I Samuel 2:12

"Feeling unique is no indication of uniqueness."
—Doug Coupland

SOMETIMES FULLY BEING ONESELF IN plain sight can be viewed as rather weird or downright odd. Our uniqueness may be labeled as strange, bizarre, quirky, or slightly peculiar. "Different" in a culture of conformity is too frequently labeled as eccentric, "out there," or unconventional. In those more humiliating moments, different can be viewed as something akin to a dork or closely approximating its close cousin, a nerd. Our uniqueness can have dramatic social implications, causing us to be the outsider, the alien, the cultural misfit, or just so weird that we're a social phenomenon entirely unto ourselves with no place within which to fit. Whatever the label, we become relegated to being the outcast.

These kinds of conclusions are quickly drawn, and judgments are recklessly rendered rather than seeing uniqueness as potentially fresh, distinctive, or entirely singular. Far too often, uniqueness is directly correlated with weirdness, dumping it into an entirely negative and typically unredeemable social sideshow. Uniqueness is reduced to oddity. It is then seen as entertaining because, face it, "odd" is entertaining. The throngs of society curiously mill about these sideshows, seeking some form of entertainment or amusement at the expense of the miracle of uniqueness. If you've had the misfortune of having been dumped in some sort of sideshow because of your uniqueness, you're seen as a permanent resident—unless you reinvent yourself and sacrifice your uniqueness as part of that reinvention. On one side, the cost to do that is astronomical. On the other side, it's deadening.

THE LOSS OF RENDERING CONCLUSIONS AND JUDGMENTS

Labels create a sharp distinctiveness that separates and excludes. The profound asset of our uniqueness becomes a crippling liability. We have these various labels slapped on our foreheads in bold type. The whole of our person is then identified by that label.

Following the brutality and ignorance of uniqueness that brands it as oddity (or worse yet, as a deficit), we are forever relegated to the sideshow of life. Oddity can be entertaining, but it's not seen as credible outside of the confines of the sideshow. It can be hilarious to watch, but its value too often ends in and with the humor. The richness of our uniqueness is then lost to us and to a world wallowing in boring but safely predictable stereotypes. In such a "lose-lose" situation, we are all diminished in ways that we may never make up.

RIGHTLY EXERCISING OUR UNIQUENESS

In a culture that embraces tolerance and diversity, let's make one point very clear. Being unique is not about taking license to be oneself and then using it as a stage to elicit attention, make some sort of controversial cultural statement, or use it as a pedestal to flaunt immoral behavior. It's not a bully pulpit from which to generate a shock factor in those who are watching us be "us." Tolerance and diversity divested of the acute insight of wisdom, the judiciousness of ethics, and the clarifying astuteness of selflessness will be tolerance and diversity for nothing other than its own agenda. Uniqueness unrestrained can cause damage unimagined.

Simply put, possession of uniqueness does not include permission to use that uniqueness with impunity to create something that we're *not,* in order to fulfill a personal agenda or fuel a social mission. That kind of uniqueness is not creative or liberating. It doesn't maximize; rather, it minimizes. It works against uniqueness to hem it in by demanding that all uniqueness look like our uniqueness. Exercising our uniqueness to press an agenda is really selling our uniqueness to sell the agenda. Our uniqueness is not a lifeless tool to be snatched up and errantly or thoughtlessly used in the service of the cause for which we choose to use it. Being authentically oneself is much more responsible and careful than that.

PRICELESS UNIQUENESS

Being oneself is about embracing a deep respect for the stunning and vibrant uniqueness of all of creation, a uniqueness that has been carefully crafted, unapologetically exercised, and fully manifested in each one of us. It's respecting that uniqueness within us not as license to be itself at the cost of everyone else around it, but as a unique resource that uniquely builds upon everything else around it. It is not a pedestal to demand tolerance of the aberrant behaviors that we take license to construct from of our uniqueness. Instead, it's a place where we bow in some soulful combination of deep appreciation and awe as we look to unearth carefully who and what we are without twisting or tainting who we are in the process. It has nothing to do with revisionist mentalities or self-decreed permission where we seize our uniqueness, plop it as some lump of clay on a potter's wheel, and methodically shape it to our designs or our likening without regard for what it really is. Uniqueness used in these ways will cease to be unique.

Uniqueness is a comprehensive expression of God's genius gloriously detonated like sweet spiritual shrapnel throughout every fiber of our being. Our uniqueness is deliberately displayed in even the slightest intonation and least inflexion of voice and action. All of that renders every one of us as unique masterpieces. Those masterpieces are liberally set about the entirety of the globe, creating a never-ending museum that never duplicates a single treasure twice.

UNIQUENESS GONE BAD

The uniqueness of our individuality under the total control of the individual is likely to be driven by selfish and self-centered agendas that will make us unique, but uniquely troubled, dysfunctional, disoriented, and distorted. The power of uniqueness in the hands of limited people with unlimited parameters is dangerous indeed. In a culture of self-determination, personal rights, and the territorial thumping of our chests to declare that we're the masters of our own fates, we take license with our uniqueness that is not necessarily ours to take.

The cultural mindset of brazen independence creates a misguided sense that we are indeed of our own making. We believe that if we don't shape who we are in the image we've determined we should have, we will have completely squandered our lives. Our mentality is that it's up to us to make "us." We think that we've reached out and formed ourselves from the dust of the earth, and that grants us permission to form ourselves right on through to the grave. It's not about creating ourselves—because we can't and we didn't. Rather, it's understanding who we were created to be and embracing the unique privilege of partnering in the development of that creation through however many years we've been granted.

UNIQUENESS WELL HANDLED

It seems that our uniqueness is not a cache of traits to be shaped by us, but understood by us. It's not to be engineered by us, but explored by us. It's not to be created by us, but cultivated by us. We do not set its agenda; we discern it so that we know enough of it to know the agenda *it* has set for *us*. Our uniqueness is a precious gift that's designed to be understood so that we can participate in making it the most that it can be, not shaping it into what we want it to be. Our uniqueness holds within it the clues and the resources that tell us who we are, why we're here, and what we're supposed to do with this gift called life.

Our uniqueness is most effectively nurtured and cultivated within moral and ethical parameters that don't inhibit that individuality as the culture assumes, but rather creates a place for us to maximize that individuality. Moral and ethical parameters keep our uniqueness pure, supple, and free from all the things that would tarnish and ultimately destroy it. Uniqueness is a priceless gift that is as fragile as fine china, as tough as fired steel, and as broadly expansive as the creative genius of God. It is a gift beyond our ability to handle, but not beyond our ability to surrender to as characteristics and features greater than us so that they will eventually become greater within us. Uniqueness surrendered and lived out in the enabling power and protective place of moral principles and ethical standards paves the way for that uniqueness to rise to unparalleled heights, to be more than we can think or imagine, and to grow far beyond the horizons of any vision we could craft for it.

Leo Buscaglia wrote, "A wonderful realization will be the day you realize that you are unique in all the world. There is nothing that is an accident. You are a special combination for a purpose— and don't let them tell you otherwise." You are unique…that's already an established reality. Amazingly, you are one of a kind. You have one and only one shot at life. So, what are you going to do with the immense gift of your uniqueness? You will cultivate or kill it. You will nurture or nullify it. You will revel in the wonder of it or revile it. You will hold it as a treasure or sell it to sell an agenda. What will you do? Consider it.

CHAPTER 23

What We Worship: The Things We Bow Down To

"You shall have no other gods before me."

—Exodus 20:3

"Every one of us is, even from his mother's womb, a master craftsman of idols."

—John Calvin

WE ALL WORSHIP SOMETHING. FOR the strong and stalwart types among us, we probably find that statement a bit pathetic—or at least somewhat unsavory. We're a little too manly and grown up for that. For the more passive among us, that statement might make us feel more subservient and possibly more used than we already felt. We already spend plenty of time bowing to our own insecurities. For everyone else, it might resonate as slightly antiquated with a dusty touch of religious sentimentality. However we respond to it, we all worship something.

The concept of worship can cut against the grain and be viewed as an action that undercuts our independence. Worse yet, the whole idea or act of worship might usurp our independence altogether, which for many us is a rather frightening proposition. Some view worship as a tossing away of our freedom, where we fling our liberties at the feet of some deity out of the hope that some sweet blessing will be lavished upon us. Worship implies an exchange of power, where we're perceived as being on the losing end.

Often, we conceptualize worship as being an act that demands our obedience and allegiance. To many, worship suggests subservience and a kind of scripted groveling. To others, it's an action that they sense is owed to something in their lives, or it can be an endeavor that draws one close to the object of worship. Some view worship as an undertaking that keeps a person humble, a reminder of their lowly place in the larger food chain called life. Regardless, we all worship something.

OUR NEED TO WORSHIP

Dorothy Thompson said that "the instinct to worship is hardly less strong than the instinct to eat." That's powerful. There's a sense of something greater woven and intricately threaded within us that demands that we worship. Benjamin Disraeli framed it nicely when he said that "man is made to adore and to obey: but if you will not command him, if you give him nothing to worship, he will fashion his own divinities, and find a chieftain in his own passions." Worship is inherent within us. It's a part of us that we can't surgically remove or blissfully wish away. We might not call it worship. We might label it as commitment, allegiance, fortitude, grit, single-mindedness, or tenacity. But in the end, it's most often worship. And most often, it's the worship of a chieftain derived from our own passions.

There's something core within us that needs something core above us. We need to believe that we're not the end of the story, because the miraculous can't find a place to set down roots in the tiny confines of our single story. If life ends with us, it ends without wonder.

Wonder is more vast than any one story and more enchanting than a million stories sown together. Life can't end with us, because it will end in the disappointment that we never found anything other than us...and we know that there's more.

So, it seems that we're always about the process of creating a thing that can be that core *thing* that we worship. We have to come up with some *thing* that somehow embodies everything that's beyond us so that we won't die having missed out on everything but us. Oddly, creating that thing gives us control over it, which would seem to defeat the whole purpose. Yet, we can't create something bigger than ourselves. However, we go right on trying to create that cherished object of worship, anyway.

In reality, we've become quite adept at it. In creating, we might ask ourselves whether we are creating just to create, or creating some object to worship. How much of our energies, our efforts, and our creativity are directed toward the creation of some little diety that's much more than simply an idea that we came up with, and is actually more about something that we can look up to? In all our scurrying about, in all our assorted investments, and in all our daily tedium, are we honestly creating some object or goal that's big enough and sufficient enough to appear worthy of our worship? Are we building a business, or creating an idol? Are we incessantly pursuing our dream, or are we crafting a deity? Has our life been spent on making the world a better place, or are we in reality attempting to fashion a better god?

WORSHIP IMPLIES A THRONE

Worship suggests that something has been elevated above everything else. There's a thing within our lives that holds that key and sacred place, the thing that we have set on the throne of our lives. The whole concept of a throne suggests that each life has a place of primacy, a central location, or point that everything else draws from and around which everything is centered. Most of us don't think about the concept of a throne, likely because such a notion is the stuff of antiquity, some object that we would associate with pomp and circumstance. That imagery doesn't really fit in our notion of our lives as we live them out in the twenty-first century. A throne is just too eccentric and off.

Yet, in thinking about worship, it seems imperative to embrace the understanding that we each have a central place in our lives that is second to none. There is that place that we carefully guard, that "hill that we're willing to die on," that part of ourselves that's non-negotiable, and that thing that we feel we simply couldn't live without. There are those places where no one's allowed and no one can touch. We have that inner sanctum, that holy of holies that's reverenced and revered. We may not think of these places quite that way, but they're there. These are our thrones.

Some "Thing" on the Throne

It would seem to follow that if we've got a throne, and we do, that something is probably on it. Therein lies the great question for each of us. What do we put on the throne? It seems that while we have a throne, we are privileged to put on it whatever we want. Things can demand that we put them on the throne, whether that be people, dreams, relationships, careers, material objects, religious beliefs, or the desire for status. Petitions for the throne can also come from painful events, disheartening failures, any of our many wounds, or a wide array of emotional issues. Things such as denial, hatred, bitterness, and revenge can all jockey for a place on the throne. Then, there are all kinds of addictions or other destructive behaviors that will want to sit firmly on the throne so that they can rule unimpeded and unquestioned.

Ourselves on the Throne

More often than not, we put ourselves on the throne—or at least that's what we think we've done. We want to reign supreme in the kingdom we call "us." We reign with an iron scepter and bow to no one. Bryant H. McGill said that "self-made men often worship their creator." That's quite frightening. Yet, the throne of our lives is such a massive and sometimes overwhelming place that we're fooled about who's actually on it. We aren't on the throne; instead, it's those things we've put there that we think of as "us." Often, we're deluded into believing that we're reigning when we're actually subservient to the people, fears, dreams, values, or agenda that we've put on it. Because we put these things on the throne, we assume that we control them. Yet, what we put in power, what we elevate to that position, will turn and control us. Likely one of the greatest deceptions is to firmly believe that we're on throne when we're not.

WHAT SHOULD WE PUT ON THE THRONE?

The throne of our lives is a powerful place. It would make crystal clear sense, then, to carefully determine what we put on the throne. Often, we're not wise enough to know exactly what that should be. Our frequent shortsightedness and hedonism are hardly suitable lenses through which to view such a choice. It's entirely feasible that anything that "we" put on the throne will in time turn on us, usurp us, use us, or possibly destroy us. It's downright certain and outright irrefutable that anything we put on the throne other than God will turn to our ill.

Maybe it's more about "allowing" something on the throne, some person who does not demand that place, but requests it. Maybe it's a relationship that inherently seeks our good over its own. Could there be something that designed us purely for itself—something that is the only natural and perfectly good fit for the throne of our lives? Is the throne of our lives custom made for something or someone like this? Anything else on the throne will surely lead to a life that serves the agenda of the throne-sitter rather than the throne-sitter serving us. Only one thing sits on the throne on our behalf, and that one thing is the One and Only God. So, who's on your throne?

Simple Truths for Profound Wisdom

CHAPTER 24

Common Sense: Having Lost All Sense

"For wisdom will enter your heart, and knowledge will be pleasant to your soul."

—Proverbs 2:10

"I can never fear that things will go far wrong where common sense has fair play."

—Thomas Jefferson

COMMON SENSE IS A COMMON phrase that is in reality far from common. To add insult to injury, common sense also seems to weigh in a bit light on sense as well. It might be proper to say that common sense is neither common nor does it make much sense these days. Today, common sense commonly lacks sense, and we are the poorer for it.

Some things in life should simply *be* without any thought about whether they should be. We would define those as the common things. If we tinker with the idea of "common" for a moment, it would imply something that just *is* because it has a place in life that's uncontested, blatantly obvious, globally useful, intrinsically beneficial, and as cleanly natural as sunshine and rose petals. *Common* defines those things whose existence we simply presume without questioning what they are or what role they play. They just are, because they're supposed to be and we accept them as such.

COMMON SENSE

It seems that common sense should be common as well—or at least we would like it to be common. After all, when we apply common sense, things usually turn out pretty good. Even if we can't rightly define it, the phrase "common sense" has a nice ring to it. There's something soothing about the idea of common sense, as it seems to have some reliable, guiding quality to it that's much more likely to insure a good outcome. Common sense seems to bring a sure and steady compass to situations that are short on compasses. It seems to be the thing that will not fail us when all the craftiness, shrewdness, cunning, and presumed brilliance of men fails. Common sense is the spotless and orderly notion that we smile at with a kind of soothing and pleasantly simplistic agreement.

Common sense implies a cup of wisdom, a dash of discernment, and a dollop of intellectual acumen that's blended clean and translucent. It's clarity in chaos and focus when all else is frantic. It suggests the direct application of life experience, gently hemmed in by intuition and held fast by reason. Common sense is the best of our senses refusing to react to the worst of our fears. It appears to be a culmination and consolidation of the best of our experiences that in combination are sufficiently adequate to overcome the worst of who we are.

THE ABSENCE OF COMMON SENSE

The absence of common sense seems in large part to be related to the fact that we tack so much stuff on to it, cut so much stuff out of it, or painfully contort it to the point that we're not certain what we're left—and it's probably nothing even remotely close to common sense! We're prone to nip, tuck, tinker, and toy with it until it's a whole lot less to common sense and a whole lot more senseless. Common sense then gets unrecognizably blurred—or worse yet, it gets entirely lost in our tinkering.

What's problematic is that once we've done all of that stuff to common sense, we think that what's left over is still common sense. In fact, we often think that we've refined it to the point that it's tight, clean, and logically invincible. In reality, common sense is lost to the point that we don't even recognize that what we've got after messing with common sense is anything but common sense. We've got our own derivative of reality that no longer makes any sense.

But we go ahead and treat it like common sense anyway. The obvious and natural progression is that we act on it, thinking that it's common sense. The repercussions are that we end up acting on some idea or conviction that's likely distorted by our agendas or shaped by whatever the cultural bias is. The result? We do incredibly stupid things while applauding ourselves for how smart we are.

Ralph Waldo Emerson said it well when he wrote, "Common sense is genius dressed in its working clothes." George Bernard Shaw put it another way when he said, "Common sense is instinct. Enough of it is genius." Common sense is the stuff of simple man's uncluttered instinct simply applied to the challenges and problems that we're facing. Instinct is all of our life experiences pooled together that gives us a sense that a decision or an action is right or wrong, good or bad, constructive or destructive, wise or not. Common sense, then, is simply using that instinct, refusing to convolute it by engaging in tangled complexities, and doing nothing more than directly applying it to our situation as our instinct tells us to apply it.

If that's the case, then why is common sense so incredibly uncommon? Common sense would suggest that common sense itself is contaminated and distorted by things that dramatically diminish or altogether destroy common sense. We bias it and distort it through a number of means that undercut it and render it largely anemic. In doing that, we rob it of its simplicity, sully its purity, and then strip it of its effectiveness. We make decisions based on whatever we're left with, and the end product is typically a handful of outcomes reeking with the rancid stench of stupidity.

Authentic Common Sense Is Free of Prejudice and Bias

Common sense is a frankness that's not convoluted by prejudice, bias, special interests, personal demands, self-centered motivations, self-seeking agendas, or any of a thousand things that twist it to something rank and spoiled. Those things cloud common sense to the point that it's so mucked up that we can't see in it, through it, or around it. In reality, common sense is a blend of truth and fact untainted by any agenda that would dilute or skew it. It's clean and transparent, uncluttered by all of the muck and mire that we rigorously pump into it.

What makes common sense so uncommon is that we contaminate it with all that stuff. We have a difficult time setting our agendas cleanly apart and maintaining some disciplined degree of objectivity. We don't get that common sense has a voice of its own and that voice is *not* our voice. What we adamantly listen for is our voice, our opinions, our sense of what should be. What do we think about this, that, or the next thing? What are the pros and cons that we can weigh out to weigh in our favor? We tend to like to hear ourselves talk anyway, so when we hear our own voices, we typically like what we hear. Because we like what we hear, we assume it to be common sense, and we act on it as such.

Common sense is not our voice. It's the voice of life experience. It's the voice of uncompromised truth and hard fact. It's the voice of a guiding conscience that whispers or sometimes screams in the back of our heads. It's the voice of a vastly superior God who is far greater than who and what we are and who speaks simple truths that are so clean that we can't even apprehend them in the sludge of our own minds. Whatever common sense is, it's *not* our voice. So, if we're listening to hear what we're saying, we're not listening for common sense.

AUTHENTIC COMMON SENSE USES KNOWLEDGE AS WISDOM

Despite the fact that it's pretty clear and simple, we somehow have the need to analyze, decipher, scrutinize, probe, inspect, dissect, and then review it all in retrospect. If we don't go through this gargantuan process, we feel that we're not being entirely responsible and thorough. In this cumbersome process, the intellectual acumen takes it all in a thousand different directions that are then further skewed by our own biases. In the end, common sense is killed and swapped out with an intellectually shiny and impressive but irrelevant and utterly off-base idea or concept. Once we get to this place, it's all so messed up that we typically can't even backtrack well enough to find the place where we left common sense dead and buried.

Robert Green Ingersoll said that "it is a thousand times better to have common sense without education than to have education without common sense." Common sense is not learned in academia. Rather, it's a consistently reliable sense gained by raw, hands-on, day-after-day experience where we get slapped and slugged. Common sense is gained in the rough and tumble of life where we get beat, bruised, belittled, betrayed, and battered. It's standing up after we've been pummeled, shaking ourselves back to some level of consciousness, and asking, "What did I learn from what just happened?" That which we learn, we add to our base of preexisting knowledge. It's the pooling of all those experiences and bringing them to bear on our situation that's the raw fiber of common sense.

THE VALUE OF COMMON SENSE

Common sense is a whole lot more valuable then we might think. There is something inherently grounded in common sense, an unsullied truth that resonates with the facts and the realities of whatever we're facing. It keeps things on track, focused and balanced. It directs correctly and in a manner that brings relevant solutions that are effective even in seemingly implausible and impossible situations. Common sense takes the confusion that we tend to create and develops a clarity that sometimes seems too simplistic to be real.

Yet, common sense can have tremendous value. Re-evaluate your thought processes. Reconsider the impact of both your own mind and all the sordid messages impressed upon you by the culture. Get back to the basics and you'll find that life often has a stunning clarity that was stunningly missed.

CHAPTER 25

Consequences: Trying to Sidestep the Inevitable

"Cast your bread upon the waters, for after many days you will find it again."

—Hebrews 11:1

"Everybody, sooner or later, sits down to a banquet of consequences."
—Robert Louis Stevenson

ISAAC NEWTON'S THIRD LAW STATES that "for every action there is an equal and opposite reaction." Put more simply, there's a consequence to the stuff that we do. We all know that. Norman Cousins wrote that "a human being fashions his consequences as surely as he fashions his goods or his dwelling." We clearly fashion our consequences, and we do that by making the choices that we make. It naturally follows that when we make a choice, we've also set up a consequence—a response to whatever choice we've made. We'd much prefer to live in a world where we could choose the consequence or choose not to have a consequence at all. Yet the consequence of thinking we can choose—or better yet, eliminate a consequence—is that we'll be blindsided by some sort of consequence that we'll likely find unpleasant.

Mark Twain came at consequences in a somewhat humorous way when he wrote, "The man that sets out to carry a cat by its tail learns something that will always be useful and which will never grow dim or doubtful." There are consequences to every choice that we make. We experience the consequences of our own choices, as well as the consequences of the choices of others. It doesn't matter who makes a choice; there will be "an equal and opposite reaction," or what we call a consequence. Some choices are fairly smart, and some choices are downright stupid and straight-up ignorant. Whatever the choice, the hope is that we'll learn from the consequences because the consequence is inevitable.

OUR APPROACH TO CONSEQUENCES

We may approach consequences in a variety of ways. We might attempt to ignore the reality of them; after all, ignorance is bliss. We might try to write our consequences off as not too big of a deal and not as bad as they might appear at first blush. We might play them off, find humor in them, give them a face-lift so that they don't look so ominous, blame others for them, try to wiggle out of them, attempt to render them as irrelevant by claiming them to be unfair, or actually position ourselves to embrace and engage them. We can fear them, laugh at them, be respectful of them, marginalize them, plan for them, or plan to ignore them. Whatever we do with consequences, they're there, and we know it.

OUR PLAN OF ATTACK

In considering the potential consequences of the choices we're contemplating, one would think that the consequences would cause us to consider, or possibly reconsider, our choices. In other words, the consequences should have a rather large hand in determining what choices we're going to make. It would seem altogether logical and reasonable to weigh out of the consequences of our choices before we make them and then adjust our choices to minimize or marginalize the consequences. Simple wisdom and basic common sense would suggest that our plans should be shaped not by the plans themselves, but by the outcome of those plans.

But quite often, we do the "tail wagging the dog" kind of thing. We don't want to modify or sacrifice our choices. We rather like our ideas, or we've warmed up to some plan to the point that it's pretty comfy and cozy, so we want to stay there. We don't want to compromise or make alterations. We become angry or put out that there are any consequences in the first place. How much further could we get if we didn't have to deal with the stupid repercussions? We embrace some sort of entitlement that says we should be able to do what we want to do without the punitive effects of some pesky consequence. We want the freedom to fully leverage the plan and completely level the consequence. To put it bluntly, we want what we want without irritating obstructions.

So our orientation is not to alter our choices, but rather to attempt to alter the consequences of those choices. It's an odd, warping kind of turn where we intellectually bend ourselves around some corner where the consequences are seen as an annoying impendence and therefore subject to removal if we can pull that off. It's an effort to remove, or at least minimize, the consequences so that the choice remains uninhibited.

THE POTENTIAL COST OF REMOVAL

At first blush, attempting to navigate away from consequences or minimizing their impact doesn't sound so bad. In certain situations, there's wisdom in this course of action. Seatbelts reduce the consequences of an accident. Fire sprinklers reduce the consequences of a fire. Insurance reduces the consequences of some major life event. Certain types of training can reduce the consequences of life-threatening situations.

However, in many instances we might be very wise to ask what the consequence of removing the consequence might actually be. Could it be that the consequence we're trying to remove is actually the non-negotiable next step in achieving our goals rather than an obstacle to those goals? Is it possible that a strong and sturdy life is built on consequences as much as it is on successes? Are consequences far greater teachers than any achievement could ever hope to be? In fact, can we really get anywhere at all without a handful of consequences playing an indispensable role in getting us to our destination?

Additionally, in attempting to remove certain consequences, are we unknowingly setting ourselves up for even greater consequences? Is it conceivable that the biting nature of some consequence might provide us a potentially critical redirection, causing us to recoil and jump back from what might have been a terribly devastating consequence? Is it reasonable to assume that the jarring nature of a particular consequence might be the very thing that strong-arms us away from making a poor choice that we didn't see as poor? *Are consequences the very things that save us?* We might want to ask these things because we're likely to miss the potentially important impact of the very consequences that we're trying to avoid. However, the impact of those consequences will certainly not miss us.

THE DANGEROUS REMOVAL OF THE CONSEQUENCES:
CHANGING VALUE SYSTEMS

Sometimes, we can reduce the consequences by reducing our values. Why not? Often what's at stake in a choice is our moral and ethical value system. If we didn't care as much, or if we just backed our conscience off a bit, or if we were a bit less fundamentalist in our ethical or moral orientation, the consequences wouldn't seem quite as bad. So, if we just loosened up a bit and expanded our ethical boundaries up and out a little, the consequences wouldn't seem quite so harsh.

So, we sacrifice our values to reduce the consequences. We shave off a whisper-thin bit of our ethical and moral orientation just enough to keep our ethics and morals intact, allowing ourselves just enough wiggle room to maneuver around a consequence. Simply put, the problem is that there's a consequence to the action of compromising our values, and it's much bigger than the consequence we're attempting to avoid.

LEGISLATE IT AND LEGALIZE IT

Sometimes the consequences occur because the action is illegal, or at least partly illegal. So, why not make it legal? There are many instances where our culture moves to legalize an entire array of actions and behaviors so that the consequences are legislatively removed. Making something legal doesn't necessarily make that "something" right. However, too often we blindly correlate the two, assuming that if it's legal, it must be okay. As is often the case, legal does not necessarily equate to legitimate. So, one way to effectively eliminate consequences is make the action or the choice legal.

IGNORE IT

Ignoring a consequence is based in the somewhat shaky and rather dim hope that the consequence will go unnoticed and simply disappear. If we ignore anything long enough, it's likely to simply dissipate and eventually vanish with no one being the wiser. Pay something no mind and it will not be paying us a visit—that's what we tend to think. When we do this, we run the risk of the consequence coming back to bite us. However, the greater pay-off in believing that the consequence will actually disappear, the more tantalizing it is to go ahead and take the risk of getting bit. Newton didn't call his third law a "law" for nothing. We *will* get bit, and the teeth of what bites us are often quite large.

Consequences as Cautions

We would be wise to see consequences as a fortuitous caution regarding the choices we're considering. They are life's precious premonitions, telling us what will happen before it happens. They raise a red flag that can be instrumental in keeping us safe from our own blatant stupidity and reckless selfishness. Consequences are often the road sign telling us that the bridge is out. The problem is that we're often lying at the bottom of the ravine before we recognize the value of the sign. So, do you want to ignore consequences, circumvent them, or give them your fullest attention and utmost consideration? Your choice will determine the consequences.

CHAPTER 26

Experience: Living, Saving, or Forgetting

*"Israel served the LORD throughout the lifetime of Joshua and of the elders who outlived him and who had **experienced** everything the LORD had done for Israel" [emphasis mine].*

—Joshua 24:31

"The difference between school and life? In school, you're taught a lesson and then given a test. In life, you're given a test that teaches you a lesson."

—Tom Bodett

EXPERIENCES. WE ALL HAVE THEM. Good, bad, or indifferent, we all have an ever-increasing multitude of experiences that we simply chalk up to "experience." Whether the road has been long or short, bumpy or smooth, uphill or downhill, oddly inverted or perfectly flat, precarious or pleasant, our roads are filled with a wide array of experiences. Experiences are the things we soak up and find sticking to us as we move through life. They are sometimes gently noted in the lightest pastel wash across the canvas of our hearts and sometimes scrawled in indelible ink down the pages of our minds. Some of our experiences have left us with jagged contusions that ooze emotional blood sopped with tears. Other experiences are soft, warm, and comfy cozy. All of us have experience with experiences.

So, what do we do with these experiences? When you've got so much of a certain thing, you've got to do something with it. Sometimes, it seems that we methodically catalog these experiences into some sort of historical file out of some element of respect for our own history. Or we vigorously work to erase them out of our lives if they're less than pleasant or downright toxic. Sometimes we just let them sit there in this river of time and become increasingly fuzzy and indistinct as that river draws them farther and farther away from us.

In some cases, they become the precious heirlooms of our own histories, places that we very much like to visit from time to time as they're filled with warm and nostalgic memories. In other cases, we refuse to admit that they were part of our histories at all; we do some rigorous historical revisionism because we find the experiences too painful. Sometimes, we don't want to permit them into our lives because they don't fit into the framework of whatever we're creating and shaping our lives to be. In order to solve that problem, we pick up a thick red pen and do some aggressive editing.

We tend to negate or neglect the fact that our experiences are precious building blocks filled with precious building materials. Too often, we fail to consider that experiences are a whole lot more than events or happenings that we simply catalog, erase, leave to the ever-distancing river of time, store as the stuff of nostalgia, or editorialize. Experiences are the things that life graciously places right in our laps that are generously jam-packed with every resource we will ever need to build every aspect of our lives.

Experiences shouldn't be deemed as irrelevant and less than vogue because they're old or dated, sitting somewhere in the dusty catacombs of our past. Experiences aren't just memories of the past.

They are the foodstuffs of our future. Experiences are the rugged, reliable, completely unmatched, and wholly pure raw materials that drill our foundations deep, and thrust our lives up and out. Nothing else possesses any kind of richness that can even come close to replacing them. Our experiences are so much more than what we've allowed them to be.

EXPERIENCES AS PACKAGES

The key lessons within our experiences tend to be timeless, although we seem to date them anyway. The integral stuff tucked within our experiences is always fresh. The experience itself might become outdated, but the experience is simply the thing that carries the lessons and the life truths. To look at it another way, it might be helpful to view the experience as the package that transports the lessons and life truths. The things that are nestled deep in the experience are really only being delivered by the experience. Therefore, the package might age, but the contents are forever timeless and eternally fresh.

With that being said, the obvious question is simply this: what do we do with our experiences? Without question, they contain lessons and life truths that are sometimes remedial and basic. At other times, they're potentially transforming and jarringly life-altering. So, do we discard them like some piece of junk mail randomly delivered into our lives, or do we take the time to unearth the lessons and life truths that they contain? It might be worth taking a moment to consider a few ideas that will assist us in squeezing the precious nectar out of every experience:

LIVING THE EXPERIENCE

Living the experience involves an aggressive and intentional incorporation of lessons and life truths. It's about the sweaty rigor of digging out and unearthing the gems that reside in the experience so that the experience itself delivers vibrant lessons and vigorous strength to our lives. To effectively dig out and unearth the gems, we have to *live* the actual experience, because it's in living the experience that the lessons and life truths within the experience become starkly clear and vibrantly evident to us. In living the experience and paying careful attention to the living of the experience, the lessons and life truths breathe and live and speak to us with a voice of their own. Rather than being sterile concepts, nice ideas, or admirable principles, they take on a life that dramatically accentuates them. They are then able to intersect all of our lives with all of their life.

Living an event or series of events is far different from being told about them. Sometimes, we hold our experiences at arm's length, never letting them get close enough to become something other than a lesson. We often manage experiences—or seek to manage them, anyway. Management is not bad; it is often quite appropriate and called for. However, we need to ask if we manage the life out of the lessons that the experience is providing us.

Saving the Experience

Sometimes we seek to save the experience. Saving implies parking the experience somewhere for retrieval at another time. It's based on the assumption that the lessons of the experience are either premature and therefore a bit too early, or they've arrived a tad bit late and therefore might be of some value at another time. Saving the experience grants it credibility and some measure of value, but not at this time. There's an assumption that we'll come back to it when time, space, and possibly need permit.

Saved experiences have a very short shelf life. Often the relevance to our present situation rapidly deteriorates as the situation changes or things move on to the point of the lesson becoming meaningless. The lesson will likely have a larger life value or principle that goes far beyond a given situation and is therefore timeless. Yet, its application to a specific place in our life may well be forfeited because we shelved it. Therefore, whatever gift it held for our future, that gift is likewise diminished or possibly lost.

FORGETTING

Then there are situations where the experience is simply forgotten. In far too many cases, the lesson is forfeited and lost to the misty backwaters of our minds and our lives. We just didn't let it register. We somehow didn't see the experience in the first place, or maybe we saved it and forgot it after we saved it, or we simply discounted it as pabulum and fluff, therefore paying it no mind in the first place. Maybe we saw it as a fluke and more the stuff of happenstance, believing it had no real relevance to our lives. Or maybe we're so captivated by all the demands of our lives and whimsy of our minds that the experience just dropped off the edge of our consciousness.

By nature, we tend to forget. Frequently, forgetting is really about prioritizing. The things we forget are typically things we've determined are not worth remembering in the first place. We figure they're not worth remembering because we really haven't understood their value. Often, we see the experience, but we don't see the lessons and life truths nestled deep in the experience. We see the package but not the pearls. We forget, and in the forgetting, we forfeit the treasures. Sadly, in the forfeit is great loss.

YOUR EXPERIENCES

So what of your experiences? You would do well to mark this day as the day that you will no longer forfeit the lessons and life truths in the experiences that come your way. Whether your experiences are joyful or painful, all of them have precious lessons packed away in them. Take stock of your experiences, painful or otherwise, and allow yourself to grow dramatically from them.

CHAPTER 27

Fill 'er Up:
It's Never Lasting

"But God said to him, 'You fool! This very night your life will be demanded from you. Then who will get what you have prepared for yourself?'"

—Luke 12:20

"The best things in life aren't things."

—Art Buchwald

DID YOU EVER THINK ABOUT the fact that we're always going back for more? Have you ever thought about the way we do something only to wind up doing it again? We always need more of this and more of that. Everything we acquire runs out. Whether things run out slowly or rapidly, predictably or unpredictably, in a manner that's satisfactory or unsatisfactory, everything runs out. When things do, they incessantly nag at us to fill them up again so that they can run out again, and then they hound us to fill them— again. There are few things obtained that don't need to be obtained again at some point. It's circular; we do things or get things knowing full well that we're going to have to do them and get them again. It never ends.

THE REPETITION OF REPLENISHING

We never go to the grocery just once. We never pull into the gas station one time and call it good. We never pay our utility bills and breathe a sigh of relief because that's the last time we have to do that. We never cut the grass and in doing so gather all of our friends around us to celebrate this once-in-a-lifetime event. We never take a shower and emerge thankful that we never have to submit ourselves to that again.

What is it about this world that it never meets our needs permanently? Why is it that we have to repeatedly do things over and over and over? The refrigerator gets empty. The gas gauge in the car is always in a free-fall toward that irritating "E." The utility bills come every single month, year after year. The grass grows as soon as we cut it. And if we're wise and like our friends very much, we shower frequently. Very few things are a one-time deal or a one-shot affair. Our lives are spent repeating activities and repeatedly obtaining resources to meet our fundamental needs. It's a never-ending cycle. Have we ever taken the time to ask why?

THE DULLING OF DETERIORATION

As we know, the oddity of life is that nothing is permanent. But taking that thought one ugly step further, not only are things not permanent, things constantly deteriorate as well. Everything's always on the fast track to falling apart. We have the words *new* and *old* in the English vocabulary because of an unchangeable principle that's as old as time. That principle is that things deteriorate, decline, weaken, wane, fade, and fail with the passing of time. Every second that ticks off the proverbial clock causes everything to be nudged one second closer to that ever-awaiting state of dilapidation. There's all this endless upkeep on any number of a thousand things that we own. All the meticulous upkeep is nothing more than our cosmetic efforts to offset the certain eventuality of dilapidation and death. Paint peels. Metal rusts. Cement cracks. Pipes become brittle. Upholstery fades. Food spoils. Wood rots. It all deteriorates.

Even the very bodies that we live in age and decay; the "fountain of youth" is only a nice tale spun by a misty-eyed dreamer who realized that everything is permanently temporary. Sure, we try to give it the appearance of permanence through Botox, plastic surgeries, liposuction, various laser procedures, the bleaching of our teeth, and hair transplants. Yet the appearance of time turned back is not time turned back. Robert Brunstein put it uniquely when he said, "The invention of film has given our generation the dubious advantage of watching our acting heroes deteriorate before our eyes." The very bodies that we inhabit decay right as we live in them.

A Vision We Can't Sustain

Additionally, we seem to create lives that reflect our desires. Whether those desires are for wealth, homes, success, security, material objects, or any number of things, we're set on building them out of the temporary stuff of this world. Therefore, these things that we create and build are likewise temporary. We cannot build something permanent from the raw material of the temporary. Other than the wonderfully eternal part of ourselves, everything we lay our hands on is temporary. In building, acquiring, or amassing it, we're setting the stage for a time when we'll lose it.

Therefore, everything that we grab hold of is also a prisoner of deterioration. We can build our dreams in whatever manner that we choose to build them and lay massive foundations to sustain them, but there's something of permanence completely lacking in them. We can insure them, rustproof them, set up trusts to sustain them, lock them in vaults, and create wills to manage them long after we're dead and buried, but they will eventually deteriorate and be lost. It's as if we're trying to create things that are lasting in a world within which nothing lasts. It seems that we're trying to create something, or maybe replicate something that this world simply can't sustain.

This causes us to craft feeble images of some larger or more inaccessible object that seems to be a vision of the permanence that we seem to be created for. The problem is that permanence isn't something we can create or replicate, despite the best of our efforts. Rather, permanence is God's gift to us lived out in the eternity that He promises His children. As a gift, it cannot be replicated in the flat shadows that eternity casts on this world. It can only be embraced.

WE WERE MADE FOR MORE

It's odd that we have to live this hunter/gatherer kind of existence to insure the perpetuation of our own existence. We're not out in the woods hunting animals and gathering nuts anymore, but malls, shops, groceries, restaurants, car dealerships, and internet shopping sites are deluged with people doing that very thing. The stuff we obtain in the hunting and gathering only takes us a bit further up the road of our lives, but it has *no* sustaining value to it. Very few things are with us for the long haul. There's not much in this world that we can grab onto that will be there to grab onto in the distant, far-flung future. Most things serve an extremely brief role in our lives before their effects or their value are depleted, spent, and gone. In light of all that, could it possibly be that we were made for more?

MADE FOR ANOTHER WORLD?

The assumption that we might consider is that we were made for another world. While this world sustains us, it only does so through great toil and incessant endeavor. It seems that the basic essentials exist in this world, but only in a form that requires us to access them constantly when we have a much more extensive need than that. The resources of this world are ultimately expended and exhausted in the effort to sustain us. At the point that they're expended, they will have not given us enough to go on without them. With the world's resources expended, we will likewise be expended. We appear to require more than this world can give us. Are we made for another world?

Indeed, it begs the question; are we made for another world? Are we made for a world that provides us resources that have some permanence to them that matches our own? Is there a world that won't be expended in sustaining us? Is there a place where nothing ever runs dry, where nothing is ever depleted, where some infinite warehouse holds stores sufficient for an eternity of eternities? The incongruence of what this world offers and what our needs appear to be would suggest a mismatch. So, is life just this way, or were we made for another world that isn't mismatched to our apparent needs?

It's also curious that our own vision and imagination is beyond our own existence. How is it that we can visualize and create both ideas and concepts that supersede the small confines of our own existence? How is it that we can visualize some object or idea far beyond our existence if in some way, shape, or form that existence didn't really exist? How can we go beyond the confines of our world if there weren't some other world that we've drawn from because somehow a bit of it is inherent in each of us?

TRAINING FOR ANOTHER WORLD

Gottfried Keller wrote, "A human life is a schooling for eternity." Is it possible that what this life demands of us is really training for another world—maybe an eternal world? It might well be that the growth that we need to experience to maximize our enjoyment of an eternal world is to live in a world that's not eternal. And maybe we're supposed to do so as people who are in and of themselves eternal. If we are infinite beings, is it possible that we are most dramatically and profoundly shaped by the rigors of a finite existence? And could it be that the best lessons of eternity are learned in the sweat, pain, and angst of a world that has nothing of the eternal in it except us? Is it possible that, out of the loneliness of being infinite creatures in a finite world, we spend our lives trying to recreate that eternity, and the lesson is that we *just can't*? Maybe we were made for another world. It's a tantalizing and marvelous thought worth probing.

CHAPTER 28

Have We Forgotten?: Lulled to Sleep

"At noon Elijah began to taunt them. 'Shout louder!' he said. 'Surely he is a god! Perhaps he is deep in thought, or busy, or traveling. **Maybe he is sleeping and must be awakened'"** *(emphasis mine).*

—1 Kings 18:27

"A life of leisure and a life of laziness are two things. There will be sleeping enough in the grave."

—Benjamin Franklin

WE'VE HEARD THE PHRASE "DEER in the headlights." It suggests that we get mesmerized to the point that we're no longer in control of ourselves or our faculties, consumed by something external. Something bigger than us seizes our attention to the utter elimination of everything else; we're standing in the road of life about to be run over. Looking at it another way, it can be likened to the proverbial "kids in a candy shop," where some sweetly desired object captivates our attention to the exclusion of everything else. There's the "shiny object" that becomes hypnotically mesmerizing. We become so mystically enraptured by it that it becomes our total focus while everything around us free-falls into the dark shadows of our unconscious. We end up falling asleep while we're wide awake.

Sometimes, it's not about anything in particular; it's just that we don't think. Frank Clarks said that "a habit is something you can do without thinking – which is why most of us have so many of them." Simply put, sometimes we just don't think to think, and so not thinking becomes habit. Thinking evokes stuff like responsibility, the need to assemble a bunch of facts, and the mental fatigue it takes to do that. Thinking takes energy, and sometimes it's just outright irritating and cumbersome. So why not simply play the odds and just play? Thinking to think just hurts. So let's run with the wind, let our compass set itself to some mystical port of adventure, and head off! Sometimes, we just don't think to think anymore.

THE LULLABY OF APATHY

At other times, it's the relentless monotony of our lives where things keeping moseying along in just the same way they've always moseyed along, creating a hypnotic cadence that lulls us to sleep. Sometimes it's just pure choice, where we're tired of it all and just check ourselves out. At other times, it's our apathetic sense that what we do doesn't matter because everything's going to come out in exactly the same way, no matter what. Maybe Richard Stearns articulated the most tragic form of this mental malaise when he wrote, "Some people probably are becoming numb to tragedies. What we call 'compassion fatigue' may be setting in." However or whatever, it happens; we become lulled to sleep in the living of life. We sleepwalk.

THE LULLABY OF FORGETFULNESS

It's both odd and dangerous that we can totally forget critical things, important things, things that are absolutely central to our existence. It's not so much that we forget them as it is that we give ourselves permission to forget them. We become emotionally and intellectually lazy, letting our memories atrophy and our minds go flabby. We figure that fighting didn't get us that much and surrender's probably not going to get us much less. Fighting the currents of life too often puts us in the backwaters of failure. So fundamentally, we drift into a sort of cognitive numbness that engenders an apathy of the most dangerous kind: the danger lying in the disturbing fact that we're numb to the numbness as well. When we're numb to our own numbness, we've lost all ability to make anything of our lives. Most tragically, we've fully forfeited God's plan for us. Mediocrity will mark our days, kill our potential, and murder our future.

THE LULLABY OF PERMISSION

To be lulled to sleep, we give something permission to lull us. To say that we're not somehow complicit or that we had no hand in the deed is at best denial, and at worst an outright lie. I think it's important to establish that we're not just an assorted collection of victims upon which life has covertly worked its evil and dubious intent. That makes for a nice story, and it gets us off the hook, but it's hardly the reality. Rather, if we've been lulled to sleep, we were part of the whole sleepy-time process.

THE LULLABY OF LAZINESS

Most of the time, when we're lulled to sleep, we end up there because of the things that we're not doing. Most of the stuff that we're not doing is because we've chosen to do other things instead. Let's face it; we like things easy. We say we prefer challenges and that we like to "step up to the plate" and "get our hands dirty." We like to look life squarely in the face and shout the proverbial "bring it on" with some sort of bombastic chivalry which is more smoke and drama than anything else. We want to call life out and call ourselves up. Yeah, we're bold and we're brave, and we want wade into the fast rip currents of life and swim upstream. That's the idea, anyway.

Yet, all of that stuff demands boldness and energy. There's sacrifice in living that kind of life. There's persistence and determination, both of which take a toll on us. While all of that stuff takes a toll on us, it doesn't insure any recognizable kind of victory. None of our efforts come with a money-back guarantee that states that once we're bloodied and exhausted, the life of sacrifice we've chosen will hand us a golden, diamond studded trophy that makes all our sacrifices worthwhile. We're not guaranteed that crowds will cheer and roses will be tossed by the hundreds. Sacrifice often results in a price paid with no return other than the satisfaction of having given ourselves over to a belief, a need, a conviction, or a God bigger than us. And in this life, that sounds heroic and all, but it's often not what we're looking for.

THE LULLABY OF COMPROMISE

So, we become passive. We let our attention slip. We compromise our dreams and our hopes until they're so anemic that they can't get up off the floor of our minds. We while away our time listening to the musings of a world that speaks so that it can hear itself talk and pat itself on the back for what it heard itself say. We go along for the ride, and we whittle away our values so that they more cleanly fit with the world around us. We come to the point where we think that the lyrics aren't really all that bad, and that while the script was filled with expletives, it did outline some interesting cultural agendas. We figure that people are going to do some destructive stuff anyway, so our best hope is that they'll do them in moderation. And in doing all of this, we wade ever deeper into the slimy cesspool of compromise. And here in these putrid places, we're lulled to sleep.

RIGOROUS LIVING TO OFFSET SLEEP

We would be wise to choose to live life in a manner that's fully attentive. That demands maintaining a mental sharpness. It means learning and maturing, which involves the aggressive action of immersing ourselves in intellectual and academically stimulating pursuits. It means never ceasing to ask the hard questions, even though they might result in hard answers. Rigorous living means taking nothing lightly and taking nothing for granted out of a studied understanding of the preciousness of life and the immense opportunities we have within it. It's about being wise, vigilant, accountable, and responsible despite the less than favorable places that exercising those attributes might put you. It means stepping up instead of stepping down and paying the price of paying attention.

Rigorous living means just that: *living*. Living should not be confused with mere existence, which is fundamentally the abandonment of living. It means that we view the opportunity of life as a lovingly crafted gift that we are permitted to seize rather than letting it seize us. It's refusing to be passive but also refusing to be arrogant or demanding. It's living with steeled purpose and intent. Angela Monet said, "Those who danced were thought to be quite insane by those who could not hear the music." Listen to the music and dance even when most of the world is deaf. Dance until you can't dance, and then dance again. Stay awake.

It Takes Energy

Doing all of that takes tremendous effort and energy. There's nothing easy about staying awake, and there's no short cut to this kind of place. We will get expended in the process of doing it all, sometimes expended to the point that we question the rightness or at least the value of it all. But one thing is for certain—it will never lull us to sleep or create a space for that to happen. Rigorous living never involves a nodding off where we become numb to life.

Living life with attention and intentionality means that we remain sharp and coherent, which is the enemy of slumber. Rigorous living never gives the sandman of life a place to tiptoe up behind us and sprinkle a dash of his golden grains into sleepy eyes. It means looking when we don't want to look and realizing whatever ugliness we see in the looking is only life begging to be made beautiful. Such living maintains vigilance that is never lulled to a passive sleep.

Lulled to sleep: to some degree, all of us have been sung the lullabies and have dozed off. And to a large degree, we need to shake ourselves awake, wipe our eyes clean of slumber, and commit to vigilance. This is why it is said: "Wake up, sleeper, rise from the dead, and Christ will shine on you" (Ephesians 5:14). Top of the morning to you!

CHAPTER 29

Historical Revisionist: Our Fear of Truth

"Even from your own number men will arise and distort the truth in order to draw away disciples after them."

—Acts 20:30

"Half my life is an act of revision."

—John Irving

WHAT DO WE DO WHEN there's some situation that we don't like or find difficult? How do we approach the tough stuff, the things we've done or said or participated in that "stick in our craw", that "dog our steps" and are just plain revolting and downright ugly? What do we do with the less than savory stuff, the stuff that leaves a bad taste in our mouths? Where do we put the embarrassing moments, the blundering failures, the misfires, and the backfires? How do we handle the verbal slipups, the impulsive gaffes, the pathetic bungles, and the haunting bloopers that we've all had? We all have a storehouse chock full of this kind of humiliating stuff. But what do we do with it?

We've all got histories we'd prefer to forget and decisions we'd like to undo or redo. There are things we've done or been involved in that impede us and impale us, making life messy, tarnished, and less than glowing. We all have our skeletons in the closet, our dirty laundry, our "little secrets," and our less than tidy histories. There are soiled reputations, nasty habits, less than savory tendencies, awkward choices, humiliating decisions, and a conglomeration of other things that are less than tidy and presentable. We all have moments that we'd give our right arms to get rid of, and we have histories that we'd gladly pay great sums of money to erase if there was actually a way to do that. We have them, but what do we do with them?

Then, there's stuff that's not ours at all. There are plenty of things that are encumbrances to achieving our goals, irritating barriers to our agendas and incessantly relentless blockades to our ability to shape our worlds in the manner we want to shape them. There are things in life that simply don't work when it comes to achieving our objectives. We have all kinds of things that don't fit or, worse yet, are entirely and completely opposed to the achieving of our objectives— those irritating and annoying things that we'd much prefer to do without. The world is bloated and satiated with all kinds of stuff that either diminishes where we want to go or blocks it altogether. There are all kinds of things that we had nothing to do with and had no hand in fabricating that can totally screw us up.

The Standard Approach

The seemingly correct answer as to what we do with all that stuff would be to deal with these things: embrace them, engage them, or shape them in a manner that allows them to work for us. We can let them inform us, giving us information that we might have missed. We can work toward some sort of resolution, or we can let them be guideposts and warning flags that help us avoid the very pitfalls we've stumbled into before. We can see them as challenges that beckon us to wrestle with them as opportunities to strengthen our character. Or we can allow them to stimulate us intellectually as we devise strategies to bend them to our advantage or allow them to bend us to greater growth.

But these approaches mean accepting whatever it is that we're working through. It means saying, "yup, I did that" or "yup, that's part of life." It's acknowledging the existence of the struggles, challenges, mis-steps, and assorted disappointments that we're engaging. In doing that, we give that action or that reality a place in our lives that we might prefer not to give it. It means accepting its existence, which concurrently makes us responsible for it or to it. Engaging these things gives them credibility and cements them as real.

But what if whatever it is, isn't really all that nice, appealing, tidy, pliable, palatable, cooperative, or flattering? What if it's diminishing to the point that we're shrunk to oblivion, or it's debilitating in a way that's cancerous right to our core? What if the realities are such that they stubbornly refuse to let us have the outcome we would like or the solution we'd find favorable to our agendas because they repeatedly get in the way? What if they force us to an entirely different outcome that isn't appealing at all or doesn't even support the very existence of our agenda? What if things would be better if these things were simply gone?

THE GREAT REWRITE

While there are many things we can do and a variety of approaches that we can take in dealing with all of this, one simple approach is to simply rewrite whatever it is that we're struggling with. Rather than grapple with the situation or event or happening, why not make it go away? At a minimum, why not change it up enough so that it's a bit easier to handle and not quite as hard on the old emotions? Why not create our own reality by recreating whatever it is that's creating problems for us in the first place? Why not take liberty with truth, events, or history and rewrite it all in order to create our own truth, events, or history in a manner that will more effectively serve our own agendas? Or better yet, why not perform a vanishing act of sorts, whereby we clean up the whole situation and make it disappear altogether by re-writing the whole history? Why not?

As outlandish as all of that might sound, we do it all the time. Our lives are often a massive rewrite where we take pen in hand and with a sense of artistic license exercise a bit of editorial genius and make it all different. Sometimes that rewrite is unintentional, and other times it's completely intentional. We can't seem to give life permission to be whatever it's been as somehow the script just isn't quite right. It might read exactly right in citing and reciting events or situations, but it might not read well at all when it comes to supporting our agenda. So we touch it up a bit. We add a flavorful flair here, and we pen in a bit of flourish there. We change up the syntax to make it read a little better, and we change out sentences and paragraphs so it doesn't have to be read at all. We block, copy, and delete with writer's fury. We rewrite truth, history, or events, and we do that by doing a number of things:

RE-WRITING BY EXERCISING SELECTIVE MEMORY

We can choose what we prefer to remember, thereby sorting through and sorting out all the things that are less than palatable or favorable or nice. It's not about re-writing history as much as it's about editing it to the point that we rewrite it in the editing. We chalk the editing up to perspective or point-of-view in a manner that causes the rewrite to possess an air of believability because it's just how we saw it; it's how we remember it through our own lens. Sometimes we edit out honest mistakes because innocent mistakes don't really count. Or we strike out things that we feel we had no control over because we're not responsible for those things. Yet, the snippets that we retain are typically those that speak favorably of us, that recite the story in a manner that spins it in the service of some agenda rather than being true to history.

RE-WRITING BY MAKING OURSELVES THE VICTIM

This kind of re-writing is quite shrewd, leaving the situation exactly as it was, while adjusting our position in the situation. We were victims. We were set up. We were used and abused. We were placated, manipulated, fooled, cajoled, forced, had the "wool pulled over our eyes," or a million other excuses that leaves the situation in tact but tactfully removed from us. We don't rewrite the event, but we rewrite our place and our role in it. We were the unwitting and unwilling victims of circumstance or the schemes of others, having fallen prey to a situation we didn't see and didn't understand. Somebody got the best of us or painted us into a corner. We were too young to know or too stupid to care. Yeah, it all happened, but we innocently got caught up in some scheme or strategy that we didn't see coming. So we rewrite our role into something much more appealing and favorable. It is revisionism, nonetheless.

RE-WRITING BY JUSTIFICATION

Here we don't rewrite it; we employ the escapist art of justification to rewrite the nature of it. We make it okay and acceptable by justifying it as okay and acceptable. This kind of rewrite is not about re-writing the history or the event itself, nor is it about re-writing our role in the event. Rather, it's about re-writing the rightness or legitimacy of the event. We *had* to take certain actions or do certain things. There were decisions that we had no alternative in making. We were forced into a corner, we had no alternatives, or we had to choose "the best of the worst." We didn't have a whole lot to work with, and we did our best with what we had. We were more the victim and nothing of the perpetrator, so we did what we had to do. We advocate that sometimes you have to make the hard choices, which means sometimes you have no alternative but to make a bad choice. We make events or actions ethical, moral, or just when in reality they are nothing of the sort.

Re-Writing by Selfish Agenda

Sometimes re-writing is done simply because we want to do it. History or events don't serve our agenda. We're committed to some sort of cause or goal that will only be diminished or thwarted if we're truthful and honest. So we rewrite, making the event or history what we need it to be so that it doesn't obstruct our agenda. Worse yet, we re-open the lines and the syntax to serve our agenda in propaganda-like fashion. We can become so deluded in the rewrite that we come to believe the fiction of the rewrite itself. At that point, our lives become based in our own fiction and will be guided by the manner in which we write that fiction and the degree to which it's contrary to truth.

To Rewrite or Not to Rewrite?

Will we live in truth, or the truth of our own creation? Are we courageous enough to wrestle with truth, or will we fall prey to the weakness and foolishness of our own revisions in whatever form them might take? Are we bold enough to wrestle with life in whatever manner it's thrown at us or we're thrown into it? How will we live? Put down the pen, get rid of the eraser, stop the block and copy, and play the script as it truly is.

CHAPTER 30

Miraculous to the Mundane: Refusing to Lose the Wonder and Privilege

"Jesus said, 'You believe because I told you I saw you under the fig tree. You will see greater things than that.'"

—John 1:50

"The invariable mark of wisdom is to see the miraculous in the common."

—Ralph Waldo Emerson

WE HAVE THE SUPERB ABILITY to adjust to a myriad of situations or places or circumstances. The aptitude and capacity that we inherently possess to be able to adapt is quite phenomenal. Put a human being somewhere, wherever somewhere is, and he will figure out a way to make it work. We're creative and stunningly innovative. You give a human being a handful of raw resources, and he will find a way to shape it into something that makes his situation not only tolerable, but downright enjoyable.

With creativity and imagination, one single object can be turned into many objects that can serve any number of purposes. With innovation and ingenuity, we can create things that don't exist from the raw material of the things that do. With resourcefulness and originality, we can come up with stuff that people thought was impossible to come up with. "What is," is only the primal substance from which "what is possible" is culled and created. That's what we're capable of, and that ability is outright amazing.

Terry Brooks said, "Growing up, I didn't have a lot of toys, and personal entertainment depended on individual ingenuity and imagination—think up a story and go live it for an afternoon." That's the capacity and capability that we have as human beings. We can think up a life and go live it for a lifetime. We can astutely collect the various parts of the various things that lie around us, methodically mold those things into an endless array of other things, and ultimately blend them into a life that can be quite amazing and deeply meaningful. Of all the creatures on the face of the earth, we alone have been blessed with a stunning combination of unparalleled intelligence and boundless imagination. In combination, those two things allow us to take a sparse handful of *nothing* and fashion a nearly endless world of *something* from it.

DULLED MINDS

Yet, we tend to get used to things. We accumulate, and we acclimate. It really doesn't matter much what's put around us or what we're given the opportunity to experience; in time, it becomes the norm, regardless of what it is or how spectacular it might be. If we're exposed to something long enough, it will become flatly mundane. When we live with the remarkable long enough, in time becomes so remarkably ordinary that it dissipates into the unremarkable white noise of our lives.

If there's a flaw we possess, it's one where we embrace things around us long enough that they cascade from the heights of the miraculous to the flatlands of the mundane. We accommodate things sufficiently so that they become the ordinary, despite how extraordinary they might be. Therefore, the disparaging part of who we are is that we can create wondrous things that can captivate even the sternest imaginations, only to have all of them lose any pulse of the miraculous.

GETTING THE MIRACULOUS TO THE MUNDANE: SPACES AND CAGES

We have a need for everything to have a place. Everything must fit somewhere. We have to find a zone or a niche for all the things that come our way. There has to be a box for it, a specific file to place it in, a shelf to store it on, a slot to slide it into, and some sort of system that categorizes it neatly into some place from which it never moves. Compartmentalism is contagious. Everything has to have a place, and once we've determined what it is, most things are put there and never move from it again.

In fact, we're often busy preparing a place for things before they even arrive. Part of the anticipation of something showing up is figuring out where we're going to put it when it does, rather than anticipating the arrival of the thing itself. Sometimes the process of planning can kill the joy. This all creates aching problems at times because we might scrupulously prepare a place for something that never arrives. Then we've either got to squeeze something else into the slot, or grieve the loss of whatever was supposed to be there in the first place. Everything has to have a place, whether we prepare in advance or not.

There's a sense that putting something in a place domesticates it and therefore keeps us safe. Herding an animal into a corral tames it. Fencing animals in robs them of the energy of their wildness. Caging a person or an idea or a possibility degrades it to a lifeless object on display rather than a contagious force, energizing everything around it. In the taming, its character is lost and its strength compromised. Most often, the power of things rest in the fact that they're not domesticated and they're not tamed. If we domesticate and tame a dream or a relationship, we've probably stripped it of all the marvelous things that captured our imaginations in the first place. Their power rests in the unexplainable wonderment that we can engage them while fully undomesticated and wholly wild.

THE NEED FOR CONTROL

There's a warped mentality etched in our brains that suggests that if we can't fully control something, we can't fully enjoy it. If we can't control something, we have to engage it on its terms, on its ground, with its agenda. We presume that unless we mold, control, and shape our relationship with anything that we encounter, we can't possible maximize that relationship. We believe we have to be in the driver's seat in order to squeeze everything out of every experience. Therefore, all of our experiences become singularly one-dimensional as we force fit them into our bland dictates, our terribly limited repertoire, and our atrophied vision.

We can do that or at least attempt it. The miraculous in life will always be diminished if we try to cage it. The miraculous is made miraculous by the fact that we can't control it and that it refuses to be controlled. The miraculous has its own agenda, its own course, its own destination, its own purpose, and its own mind. It's miraculous because we *didn't* have a tainting or obstructionist hand in creating it. When we apply any constraints, the miraculous will become something other than miraculous. That will happen because the only thing that we will bring to the miraculous is a whole lot of *less* and nothing of *more*.

WE CAN'T STAND THE MIRACULOUS

The miraculous invites us outside of ourselves and outside of our experiences. It's daring and it's bold. It's limited only by the limitless. It's not accustomed to the reins of restraint, and it marches to the beat of its own drum. The constraint of the miraculous is simply that it won't be constrained. If it were to be, it would immediately devolve into a lifeless object that's interesting, likely curious, and probably a bit different. However, it would not be miraculous.

Probably the scariest thing of all is that the miraculous invites us along with an open invitation. The conditions of the invitation are simply that we agree to get in, sit down, hold on, and shut up. We're invited to an adventure of profound proportions, but we're not invited to control it. We're observers who are invited to join the miraculous so that we'll always know that there's more beyond what we see. Yet, too often we tell ourselves that we couldn't stand it and that it doesn't represent the moderation that we too often choose to function within. So we either attempt to control it or graciously bow out of it because we can't stand it.

We Want it Easy

Albert Einstein said, "I have little patience with scientists who take a board of wood, look for its thinnest part, and drill a great number of holes where drilling is easy." We tend to look for a strategy that's easy, and the miraculous is anything but easy. We find the point of least resistance and set ourselves down right there. In fact, the miraculous doesn't adhere well to definitions of *hard* or *easy* because it supersedes them entirely. There's the old saying that water seeks out the path of least resistance. In some way, we must be a distant cousin to water because we like to do the same thing. The miraculous invites us away from any paths of any kind, and it bids us to walk in places where there are no paths. The miraculous might be a wonderful thing, but it's demanding, tiring, and anything but easy, so we tend to shy away from it.

We Don't Necessarily Believe

Finally, we may not believe in the miraculous in the first place. We might see some things as pretty amazing, and we may even anoint them with a slight touch of the phenomenal. Yet, "miraculous" deftly elevates things beyond the explainable. It shoves things outside the realm of our understanding and puts them in a place that defies our explanations and skirts all of our definitions. We're reasonable people, after all: logical, rational, and balanced. The miraculous may not fit where we need it to fit, despite all the contorting, trimming, and tucking that we do to it. Because we can't make it fit, we must discard it as unreasonable, the stuff of fanciful tales and unbridled idealism.

There are many reasons that we make the miraculous the mundane. In those actions, we are robbed of great treasure. We can live robbed, or we can be enriched. We can throw our limitations to the wind and embrace a belief in the limitless. That single choice has singularly miraculous implications for your life.

Chapter 31

Pain to Paralysis: Coming Apart at the Scars

"That is why, for Christ's sake, I delight in weaknesses, in insults, in hardships, in persecutions, in difficulties. For when I am weak, then I am strong."

—2 Corinthians 12:10

"Mistakes are the growing pains of wisdom."

—William Jordan

THERE'S PAIN, AND THEN THERE'S intensely deep pain. We all have both kinds. We all have the pain of failed experiences, sordid disappointments, pathetic misfires, wasted opportunities, and wasted investments that we thought were opportunities. There's the pain of not being where we imagined being, of being forced to embrace dreams as more fantasy than substance, of friends in flight and fortitude forgotten. There's the pain of growing up and growing jaded, of a world devolving despite relentless efforts to reverse it all, of diminished confidence in our fellow man, and a diminished confidence when the fellow man is us. We can add to all of that the pain of watching others in pain and the pain of feeling our own pain. Then to top it all off, there's pain that we can't even identify despite our desperate efforts to do so, efforts that make whatever's hurting us hurt all the more. Yes, there's pain, and we all have it.

CORE OF YOUR SOUL PAIN

Then there's the "core of your soul" kind of pain that's entirely different. It's the kind of pain that's rarely sharp but is immensely blunt and debilitating. It's all-encompassing and aching in ways that bend our very souls and scrape out the insides of our hearts until they're empty except for the pain itself. Words utterly fail to describe this kind of pain.

This kind of pain incapacitates us with a venomous bite that's paralyzing and heart-stopping. It's exceedingly more than just being painful, as it's a level of pain that kills. It's not a straight-up obvious kind of death, but more the killing of the soul that leaves us alive while simultaneously dead. It's pain that egotistically snubs medicinal efforts, effortlessly shreds therapist skills, slices through words of encouragement regardless of how inspiring they might be, rebuffs truth, sloughs off common sense, and has no antibiotic to remedy it. It's a pain that flouts healing, that defies a cure, and that leaves a forever limp in our souls if not a condition that's more paraplegic in nature.

This kind of pain is unreasonable and terribly cruel in terms of its intensity. However, it makes sense in terms of our humanity. It seems reasonable that we would feel this way or could feel this way. There's something of depth and soul-ness about our humanity that makes perfect sense of this kind of pain. We have been fashioned with an internal vastness that's big enough to contain the massive expanse of this kind of pain.

Indeed, we are fashioned for more greatness than we can even come close to comprehending. In a sense, being unable to comprehend our capability keeps us from fraudulently defining some sort of premature line that would cause us to pull up too early and quit too prematurely. Yet that fashioning likewise fashions us for great pain, for it's in great pain that greatness is achieved. Yet, this kind of pain is typically horrific, despite the fact that the depth of it makes sense and that the very nature of it engenders great growth. We can embrace it as feasible, but we prefer to reject it as entirely too painful.

OUR NATURAL RESPONSE

When we feel this kind of pain, we would often gladly give up some of our humanity to whittle down the pain. Indeed, we are vast, but we would gladly forfeit an acre or two of the vastness within us if that would remediate some of our hurt. We appreciate growth, but often not enough to endure the pain. We can make all kinds of good sense out of our pain, but we'd still prefer not to have it, despite the benefit it might have.

Such is the intensity of the pain that we often wonder if we'll ever recover, or recover fully. We often think that if the world is capable of inflicting such pain and we're capable of feeling it, what kind of world is this, anyway? And if the world is capable of doing this to people and we're capable of feeling stuff at this depth, it's likely that the world's going to continue to hurt us because it can and ultimately will. So the whole pain thing becomes unsavory and ugly.

ACKNOWLEDGING PAIN

The first fundamental step in dealing with all of this is to acknowledge that we do experience pain and that we will continue to experience pain. Pain seems to be accentuated when we fight it as cruel, unjust, wicked, and inherently destructive. Indeed, it might be all of those things and much, much more. Yet, it's in the very act of fighting pain that we escalate pain. In reality, the battle against pain is where a significant degree of our pain comes from in the first place. Fighting pain causes pain, so why would we do that?

This is not to say that we welcome pain into our lives with open arms and loving words. It's not to say that we deliberately subject our lives to it, or not work to protect ourselves from it. Rather, it's to embrace the fact that life has its fair share of pain and we're going to experience our fair share of it. It's refusing to take the principles of fairness and justice as some kind of ethical template, as legitimate as that template might be, and affix it over our pain, because when we do, it's highly likely that our pain's going to be unjust. When that becomes painfully obvious, we rage and tantrum and fume about the injustices perpetrated upon us in some childish rant that only serves to expend more energy and amplify our pain. We will experience pain, both just and unjust. We'd be wise to accept that.

The Goal of Pain Eradication

No one likes pain—at least, almost no one. Because we're adverse to pain, our first goal is to eliminate it. There's really no other reflexive orientation that we have other than to take some sort of step to get rid of it. The natural and ingrained response when we incur pain is to react in a way that will make it stop. That action is essentially habitual. We initiate a knee-jerk response without ever even realizing we're doing it. We instinctually move to protect ourselves without even recognizing the action. It's only in recognizing that we're doing something that we can even ask why we're doing it. The largely unrecognized yet fatal flaw in a sole focus on pain eradication is that taking action to stop the pain will typically direct our efforts to the more superficial aspects of our pain rather than focusing on the deeper dynamics that are in all likelihood the major source of our pain.

The Language of Pain – Pain Is Telling Us Something

We don't take enough time to ask what pain is telling us, because we're too busy trying to get rid of it. We want to shut it up and send it away. We've long lost the language of pain. We don't see it as an indicator, a light on the dashboard of our lives, a warning siren signaling the approach of something, or a flashing red light that suggests that we should come to a full stop right here and right now. Pain is no longer a system of the body, or of a relationship, or of life that's flagging us down before we fall down. We don't see it as a redirecting sign that's telling us that the road has been washed out or the bridge is gone. We've meticulously demoted pain to being nothing other than pain, and in the entirely thoughtless demotion, we've come conveniently to assume that pain is pain only and nothing else. Pain has an important voice. Yet, we've stripped it and silenced it. Its warnings go unheeded because we don't hear them.

PAIN MAKES US AUTHENTIC

Khalil Gibran said that "your pain is the breaking of the shell that encloses your understanding." Whatever that shell is, it's solid to the point of being impenetrable. Typically, it's constructed from the composite material of our defense mechanisms, and it's fired to a steeled strength in the furnace of our previous pain. We're constantly constructing methods to protect ourselves from threats that are in some instances quite real but in other instance are products of imaginations that are fed by the real experiences of our past. Pain softens and sometimes demolishes those shells. Pain strips us raw in the sense that all the games and all the protective layers are ripped away. Pain draws us down to reality and then back up into authenticity. It's a raw and frighteningly vulnerable place to be, but it's a profound place from which to understand who we are and then to grow deep in that understanding.

EMBRACING PAIN OPENS UP LIFE

An unknown author wrote that "love means exposing yourself to the pain of being hurt, deeply hurt by someone you trust." If we refuse to risk pain or feel pain, we've shut down vast amounts of the landscape of our lives. Refusing to feel pain means that we will refuse to engage nearly all of life. We huddle in some hovel, fearful and wincing at the very thought of pain. Crouched over, with our arms wrapped about us in abject fear, we live out lives of desperate isolation. It seems that the trade-off is far too costly. If we want to live in a manner that's sold out and abandoned to living itself, we'll need to accept pain, quit trying to eradicate it, figure out what it's telling us, let it reveal the true depths of who we are, and grow in the wild concoction of it all. Feel pain and live!

CHAPTER 32

Playing with Fire: Thinking We're That Good

"[The Death of Nadab and Abihu] Aaron's sons Nadab and Abihu took their censers, put fire in them and added incense; and they offered unauthorized fire before the LORD, contrary to his command."

—Leviticus 10:1

"People who play with fire seldom strike a match."

—Unknown Author

"PLAYING WITH FIRE" . . . I think we've all heard that phrase. There's a rather cunning, albeit misguided assumption in "playing with fire" that we can get away with an action or choice without being touched by consequences. It's courting the dare, believing that we're daring enough to get away with it. Really more than that, it's an assumption that we can take a potentially dangerous risk and be either shrewd enough or quick enough to pull it off and come out unscathed. We confidently feel that we're bright enough, more than sufficiently intelligent, adequately informed, and just plain smart enough to maneuver a situation right out of the situation and into whatever situation we want it to be. We're good, and we're out to prove it. So with that thin front of embellished confidence, we play with fire.

There's a heady boldness about playing with fire that's probably less about boldness and a whole lot more about something much more shallow: arrogance. Fundamentally, arrogance is an exaggerated assessment of one's abilities. We think we're "all that" when we're not much of anything closely approximating "all that." Applying that overestimated assessment to any given task will likely result in a significantly underestimated outcome. In other words, we'll probably get burnt.

Often, we prefer to label these actions as boldness, fortitude, resilience, or even bravery, as there's something chivalrous about that kind of language. We want to be seen as valiant and gallant, as that evokes muscular images of men fearlessly staring into the face of death. Sometimes we ratchet that language up a few notches higher and refer to our actions as a calling or a core conviction. But the reality of many of our actions, as disappointing and revealing as it is, is that they're often much more actions of arrogance: generic and plain-wrapped arrogance.

And so, out of this arrogance that we've astutely and rather deftly labeled in convincing terminology, we play with fire. Playing with fire is not about the exercise of wisdom or the application of knowledge resulting in a well-conceived action. It's not about responsible thinking, although we might throw it out there as such. Neither does it have anything to do with education, pedigree, social status, or intelligence. We're just going to play with fire for the thrill of playing with fire. We do that because we think we're that good, that we're that shrewd, we're that cunning, and that we're just "all that."

THE MORPHING OF ARROGANCE

If we've decided to play with fire in the first place, we've probably come to the conclusion that we can do it and not get burnt. Somehow, arrogance tends to grow on us the more that we invite it into our lives and intellectually converse with it. There's a kind of nearly casual feedback loop where our thinking gets reinforced simply by thinking, often without us even recognizing what's happening in the process. Arrogance begets more arrogance. Soon the difficult reality of our proposed endeavor is diminished as the misguided sense that we can accomplish our mission concurrently increases. With enough time, the reality of what we're facing is reduced to some pitifully forlorn-looking lawn troll that can easily be crushed underfoot. While the mirage is increasing, our ability to effectively deal with it is exaggerated and aggrandized to inflated proportions. When these processes happen in conjunction with each other, we're on our way to being burnt.

SOMETHING TO PROVE

Sometimes playing with fire is simply to prove something we feel needs to be proven. Maybe we want to prove that we're capable, or prove that "it" can be done, or to disprove someone who said that it couldn't be done. Maybe we want to prove that there's a sure-proof way to do it, that it's not impossible, that with enough determination anything can be done, or that it actually can't done by our trying it and failing. Maybe we're trying to prove to others that we are of value despite the fact that so many people have said we weren't. Maybe we're trying to prove that very thing to ourselves. Sometimes playing with fire is an effort to prove some ability or characteristic or fact that we feel can't be proven in any other way.

RISKY REASSESSMENT

Playing with fire cajoles us into taking risks; sometimes great risks. We question natural and healthy boundaries. Playing with fire causes us to recalculate the lines in our lives and to ask ourselves if maybe we've chosen to live terribly restrictive lives that we don't necessarily need to live. Maybe we've cheated ourselves out of a possession or opportunity. Maybe we've held ourselves back from things that we deserve. Maybe we've swindled ourselves out of opportunities that look a bit erroneous and slightly criminal but hold enough good in them to perhaps offset the bad. Maybe we're living nineteenth century values in a twenty-first century world, and because we are, the world is passing us by. Maybe we're ridiculously out of date and slovenly irrelevant. Maybe we should be a little more self-centered and call it vision and see what it gets us, because it seems to be getting other people a lot of stuff.

It seems that playing with fire causes us to reassess the lines in our lives. Because of the attitude and nature of the mentality surrounding the concept, we're drawn to compromise: blatant and unapologetic compromise. We too often see it as a reassessment of sorts, a healthy re-evaluation where we take stock of ourselves and our world and in doing so re-position ourselves in order to maximize our successes. We're redrawing the lines because in our minds it's long overdue and in reality it's wise. Playing with fire is simply brazen stupidity under the guise of some other definition that makes it appear noble and daring. More often than not, it's compromise in disguise, which is stupidity in full bloom.

WHERE IT LEAVES US – GETTING BURNT

Jack Handey said, "If you ever catch on fire, try to avoid seeing yourself in the mirror, because I bet that's what really throws you into a panic." In playing with fire, we will typically set ourselves on fire. Maybe we'll just get singed a bit. Or it's entirely possible that we could be seared, scorched, or charred to a crisp. We might get flame-broiled or just smoked real well. To whatever degree it happens, in playing with fire, we will get burned. We would be foolish to ignore this red-hot reality.

Playing with fire typically leaves us burnt and living with the knowledge that we've compromised our standards. We stand charred and shamed at the same time. On the other side of the fire, we're often licking our wounds and living with the losses that were a consequence of our actions. We're quick to realize that arrogance resembles a bulldozer that we let charge down the road of our lives with no one in the driver's seat. We realize that wisdom and discernment have nothing to do with playing with fire and everything to do with the management of it, which is entirely different. We come to understand that discretion is the antithesis of impulsivity and the enemy of stupidity. We come to see that fire burns in more ways than we realized.

If we're bright enough, we blow out the burning embers that litter our hearts, our minds, and the pristine places of souls now singed. If we're mature enough, we take accountability for our choices. And if we're genuinely bold enough, we commit to learn a lesson from the flames into which we so arrogantly stepped.

ARE YOU PLAYING WITH FIRE?

You may want to ask yourself if you're playing with fire. Don't label your actions as boldness, bravery, or the manifestation of a deep and fundamental core conviction. Certainly there are actions that are a manifestation of those very characteristics. However, playing with fire embodies an arrogance that polarizes those kinds of noble actions and sets them distinctly at the other end of the continuum from playing with fire. We can't assume that we're "all that good" because if we do, we're going to get "all that" cooked.

Finally, playing with fire typically has to do with us and our own self-gratification. Messing around with fire rarely has anything to do with the betterment of others. Playing with fire is frequently all about us and our efforts to establish that we're something that we're not. Unless you want to find yourself having the experience of being roasted, you may want to rethink what you're doing and why you're doing it. It may keep you out of the both fire and the frying pan.

CHAPTER 33

Reality:
The Extent of Your
Reach

"God said to Moses, 'I AM WHO I AM. This is what you are to say to the Israelites: 'I AM has sent me to you.'"
—Exodus 3:14

"I reject your reality and substitute it for my own."
—Adam Savage

ALBERT EINSTEIN SAID THAT "REALITY is merely an illusion, albeit a very persistent one." Yet, we see reality as anything but illusion. The concept of reality is expounded upon with a rather tenacious and robust vigor as we either try to understand what it is or defend our understanding of it. Reality becomes linked with truth, so the idea is that he who holds reality also holds the truth. That makes it all the more valuable.

When we throw around the word *reality*, we assume it to mean all that's really real. We see reality as an ideal where all the fake and fraudulent has been entirely peeled away, leaving nothing but that which is true and genuine. The word *reality* suggests an idea or belief that's completely grounded, entirely true, and totally accurate. We sense it as a concept or perspective that's rock solid and unarguably the end of the story. It's where the buck stops; it's the end of the road; it's the final analysis, and it's the final word. Reality for most of us is what life was like before we added all the junk to it. It's the uncontaminated raw essence of existence. In other words, it's the untainted, untouched, unalterable truth.

SHOPPING FOR AND SHAPING OUR REALITIES

Yet, out of our indomitable need to be masters of our own fates and the captains of our own ships, we prefer to shape our own realities. Rather than have to submit ourselves to some demanding or constricting reality, why don't we either create one or find one that's a bit less taxing and a lot more flexible? Why can't reality be what we make it rather than having it make us something we'd prefer not to be? Why not seize the rudder of our lives and steer a heady course to our chosen port of call rather than heading to a place that's not our preference? Why not create our own realities so we can do that exact thing?

It's odd that we think we have the ability to wield power that we don't possess. We don't see ourselves as wonderfully privileged to be a part of this amazing journey that's been laid out before us. We miss the fact that God has meticulously crafted a spellbinding journey for us like none other. Rather, we see ourselves as being people who have the inalienable right and uncontested license to design, fashion, and form this journey from the ground up. We claim life solely as our private enterprise, and we cast it entirely in our design. Indeed, we have a strange way of taking liberty with things that we really can't take liberty with. We can be an arrogant bunch, thinking we have the ability or the right to manage things that we simply can't manage.

In some respects, it might be likened to some sort of god-complex or maybe the classic short-man syndrome. We think we're privileged enough or powerful enough to control that which we can't. One of the realities of humanity is our sense that our right to independence extends to our right to craft our lives in whatever manner we choose. That then creates a mentality that a pre-existent reality that is universal in nature and scope is an entirely unfair and unjust hindrance. The realities that we create tell us that a universal reality can't be a reality because of the manner in which it impedes us. Therefore, if we massage our minds enough to believe that a universal reality does not exist, we must create our own reality or be left with nothing.

It's not news to anyone that there are many supposed realities out there for the choosing. That's what makes this confusing. The world offers us a host of imitations that aren't crafted to fool us because of their similarity to the real thing, but are shaped to seduce us by playing to our greed. And if there's not a reality out there that really appeals to us, we can go right ahead and custom or semi-custom design our own. In reality, this does afford us the opportunity to embrace the reality of our choosing—even if what we end up embracing has nothing to do with reality.

OUR OWN CUSTOM DESIGNS

Often, reality is what we've constructed. We build out our lives and fashion our existence, sometimes carrying those tasks out in very meticulous ways, and at other times doing so in rather abrupt and less than thoughtful ways. Sometimes, we create our realities based on well laid out plans, while at other times we piece-meal things as we fly by the proverbial seat of our pants. Often times, we exercise great care because we care, and at other times we're careless because we couldn't care less. However and in whatever way we do it, what we construct stands before us looking strikingly real and credibly genuine at times. We can perform a downright convincing job of constructing an intellectual, emotional, spiritual, or relational behemoth that looks breathtakingly lifelike. The pressing question becomes, does the "reality" we've created reflect the larger realities around us? And in creating our own reality, have we forfeited real reality?

OUR SEMI-CUSTOM DESIGNS

The world around us seems like an expansive buffet chock full of imitation food. It's interesting that what we create is always an imitation of something else. Whether in whole or in part, the things that we fashion in life always borrow from somewhere else. That suggests that there must be something original, some creative point of departure that emerged from nothing but itself. Everything after that is, to one degree or another, a copy.

So we shop this massive buffet of cheap imitations, and we pick a bit of this and a bit of that. Sometimes we take things in their entirety, or we whack off or carve out the parts that appeal to us. With an armload of assorted pieces and parts, we walk out of the buffet; we take our purchases and craft them into our realities. Therefore, our realities are borrowed and integrated into some sort of semi-custom design. What we borrow is what appeals. So our intent is to create a reality that's appealing, that's nice, and that's comfy and cozy. Our semi-custom realities can be custom made to fit our personal agendas, our biases, our prejudices, our fears, and our emotional baggage. They can be fashioned to lend credence to our views, give us permission to avoid our pain, grant license to our indiscretions, allow us to live in blissful ignorance, and rubber-stamp all the choices, actions, and decisions that we want rubber-stamped.

BORROWING WHOLESALE

Then there's the ability to just borrow our "reality" wholesale. It's the "I'll take one of those" mentalities where we simply grab whatever "reality" is closest or whatever "reality" is the easiest and run with it. In doing this, we forfeit any ability to engage life as unique creations, and we become what someone else has designed. Sometimes we do this out of a compelling argument that convinces us that someone's design of "reality" is the real deal. Sometimes it just looks exceptional and shiny. Whatever the motivation, we borrow a "reality," and we park ourselves in it and on it. Typically, we never really question or scrutinize the reality of the "reality" simply because borrowing is much easier to do.

Yet, borrowing is a temporary transaction; what is taken is taken only to be returned from wherever it was taken. Whatever's borrowed goes back. There's never a permanent possession of whatever it is that we've borrowed, so it never really works itself down into the core of our souls; it's just not there long enough to do that. What's borrowed goes back. So when it comes to borrowing our realities, we don't borrow anything that's permanently fixed. Therefore, we live in a borrowed world, living a borrowed existence on borrowed time.

Real "Reality"

Anything that we presume to do will obviously be limited by our limitations. That means if our "reality" is limited to what we create, we'll end up living in a tiny world that's going to be thinly populated, sparse, dreary, and just plain flat. On our own, we cannot begin to hope to exercise a degree of intellectual acumen, emotional depth, or spiritual magnitude that could rise to even touch the hem of the realities of the world we live in. We build our finite realities instead of exploring an unrestricted infinite reality. We then spin little lives in dark caverns that we've come to believe are filled with irrepressible light, and we languish.

In reality, the question of "reality" has been bounced around throughout human history. It would appear that a hallmark of "reality" is that we didn't create it. Second, "reality" is not the product of innovation or alteration. Third, if a task or a principle is hard and demanding, it's probably closer to reality than the easy stuff. Fourth, embracing reality rather than shaping it or borrowing it is going to give us the richest and fullest life. And finally, reality is expansive enough to give us a life-long journey of endless horizons and ceaseless discovery. That kind of reality can only be crafted by the God of all realities. The "reality" is that you might want to really think about it.

Simple Truths for Profound Living

CHAPTER 34

Carrying It All: Ownership Versus "On Loan"

"Jesus replied, 'Foxes have dens and birds have nests, but the Son of Man has no place to lay his head.'"
—Matthew 8:20

"If one considered life as a simple loan, one would perhaps be less exacting. We possess actually nothing; everything goes through us."
—Eugene Delacroix

HAVE YOU EVER THOUGHT ABOUT ownership versus being "on loan"? Maybe not, at least not in the way I'm thinking about it here. "Ownership" versus seeing things in our lives as being "on loan"—they are poles apart. Each has a radically different impact on our lives. One drains the lifeblood out of us, and the other drains the lifeblood out of all that would possess us. One causes us to trade our soul for stuff, and the other causes us to trade stuff to regain our souls. One makes us subservient to maintenance, and the other subjugates subservience in order to maintain our freedom. One occupies the whole of our time, while the other keeps our time wholly unoccupied. One fetters us, and the other frees us. Indeed, they are poles apart.

Owning Versus a Carrying Out a Task

Owning something and simply carrying out a task are two entirely different things. The carrying out of a task holds us accountable to completing the task. It's about getting the job done, achieving a particular goal, and bringing an undertaking to a conclusion. It's about recognizing that we have a defined place and a clear role along with others who also have a place and a role. It's about completion of a task in a joint, cooperative effort that leads to an ultimate conclusion. When it's done, our job is over.

On the other hand, when we own something that's not ours to own, we not only assume responsibility for the completion of the task, but we also assume responsibility for the repercussions of all the stuff related to task itself. The implications are massive. We take on everything. We own the completion of the task, everything involved in the task itself, as well as all the sordid repercussions of the task. The size of the whole thing becomes enormous. We walk around weighed down with responsibilities or obligations that are not ours to carry, bearing all the implications of ownership when we really don't own any of it. And what moves us to assume ownership of what's not ours to own is typically the sense that what we're doing defines us. Therefore, we have to own it in order to have sufficient power to insure that it's successful.

Doing to Ownership

We often assume a gradual ownership of anything that we do. There's a kind of "slight-of-hand" transition from doing something to owning what we're doing. Somehow, the process of actually engaging in some task causes us to develop a sense of ownership over the task. The more time and effort we put into some task or endeavor, the more it becomes an extension of us. Things move from being simple, inanimate objects to becoming things that have a part of our life infused into them. Whether they're large or small, we leave a piece of ourselves in whatever task we perform or decision we make. Therefore, the more we invest in something, the bigger the piece of *us* we leave embedded in that thing. The more it becomes an extension of us, the more we sense that we somehow own it. Most often, that transition is so subtle that we move from doing something to having a sense of owning it without even knowing that the transition took place. Yet, the impact of the transition is profound whether we're aware of the transition or not.

Doing to Ownership – Defining Us

This exaggerated sense of ownership becomes increasingly powerful because there's so much of us in the task that we've allowed this thing to somehow define us. It's not about a task anymore, not even close. Now it's about our identity, our sense of self, our worth, our value, our reputation, our abilities, or our sense of competency, among other innumerable things. We have become so intimately identified with the task that it becomes some kind of mirror that reflects we are or who we aren't. It's no longer about the goal of completing a particular objective, it's what the completion of this objective says or doesn't say about us. Who we are hinges on it. We grant it a massive amount of power to define us and to determine our value.

Probably the most impactful thing that a task or goal does is define our limitations. Whenever we do something, that thing puts our limits right out on public display. What we can and can't do is plopped front and center for whole world to see, so it had better be good. So we strategize and ask, just how big can we make it? How unique can we design it? Can we take it one or maybe two steps further than anyone else ever has? How far can we push the envelope, how far can we press our luck, and how far is far enough if far enough is never enough? What we do defines and broadcasts either the limitations or limitlessness of who we are, so we'd better make it big and wide and deep and tall and outright ginormous.

We begin to own the task because of the terribly critical things the task says about us.

We naturally move to the point of owning the task because the completion of it is has become critical to how we view ourselves and how others view us. It *has* to get done, because not getting it done says bad things about us. Simply playing a role may not give us adequate power to insure success. Owning the task gives us a lot more leverage to force whatever it is we're doing to success so that we are a success...or so we think. Owning it gives us more power to make it work, make it run, make it fly, make it float, make it profitable, make it huge, make it loud, or make it whatever we need to make it. And if we end up being successful, owning the task makes the success about us...or so it appears.

WHAT DO WE REALLY OWN? OWNERSHIP VERSUS POSSESSION

What do we actually own? That's a philosophical kind of question. I would like to think that, in reality, we own nothing. Possession and ownership are two very different things. We can possess many things yet own nothing. Ownership implies that we hold something permanently; that it's exclusively ours alone. As Job said in the Old Testament, "Naked I came from my mother's womb, and naked I will depart." There's no ownership in that. If there were ownership in the truest sense of the word, these things would somehow go with us as part of our belongings. From the womb to the grave, we possess many things, but there's no permanence in the possession; in other words, we don't possess anything sufficiently to take it with us. As Queen Elizabeth I put it, "All my possessions for a moment of time." We don't own, we possess. And that possession is only for a moment.

THE INFERIORITY OF OWNERSHIP

Ownership typically implies that we manage things for our sake, to enhance our security, to achieve our goals, to insulate us from whatever we feel we need insulating from, and to maximize our comfort. It means that we utilize these resources with the intended outcome being our bottom line, whatever we determine that to be. Ownership results in a specific style of management that is focused on our gain and maximizing our profit through the use of these resources. Any benefit to others is sparsely siphoned off through whatever we've gained.

THE SUPERIORITY OF "BEING ON LOAN"

Ideally, when we possess things as being "on loan" rather than owning them, we manage them differently. First, we manage out of the belief that we have a responsibility and are accountable to whatever or whoever loaned these things to us. Second, we manage in a manner that makes the most of the things themselves, that maximizes the things that have been loaned to us simply for their sake and out of our respect for the privilege we have to enjoy them. Third, we manage to benefit others to whom these things will someday be loaned as they eventually pass from us to them.

THE BENEFIT OF SIMPLY "BEING ON LOAN"

In ownership, what we own in reality owns us. You may want to think about that. Our lives tend to revolve increasingly around the collecting, managing, maintaining, and protecting of what we own. Our lives are given over to this massive management task, and ultimately, we become consumed in and by the task. We blithely allow ourselves to be consumed, assuming that that's simply part of the responsibility of ownership. Yet, at what point does the management of that which we own turn to enslavement, which in reality causes us to *be* the possession rather than being the one *in* possession? That's not an idea that's really thought about because we prefer to embrace the soothing illusion that we're really in control. Yet, we're not.

In viewing things as being "on loan" to us, we're freed from the chains of ownership. We're about the business of management out of responsibility to the one who loaned these things to us, to make the most of the talents or resources that have been loaned to us, and to manage these things in order to pass them on—because we can't hold them. Doing these very things implants within us a wonderfully strong sense of identity, as well as generating a profound sense of worth and value. Who we are and what our worth is becomes entirely manifest and repeatedly affirmed when we live this way.

In the end, the very things that we sought by seizing ownership are fully met by simple possession and actively managing everything as being "on loan." As Orison Marden stated, "He only is rich who can enjoy without owning." It's freeing and fulfilling way to live.

CHAPTER 35

Dad's Workbench: There's a Tool for That

"All Scripture is God-breathed and is useful for teaching, rebuking, correcting and training in righteousness, so that the servant of God may be thoroughly equipped for every good work" [emphasis mine].
—2 Timothy 3:16-17

"We shall neither fail nor falter; we shall not weaken or tire . . . give us the tools and we will finish the job."
—Winston Churchill

"THERE'S A TOOL FOR THAT." I can't tell you how many times I heard Dad say that. And in the oddity of life, no matter what task we had to do, there was always a tool for it—not just some cantankerous tool to force fit a situation, but a specific tool. Someone, somewhere, at some time had faced the challenge we were facing and had designed a tool to get it done with a fair amount of ease and a significantly reduced amount of frustration and stress. Someone had faced that fact that a tool didn't exist for a particular job and came up with one. Tucked somewhere in one of the many crevices of the larger cycle of life, the smaller cycle of building a tool for every job was being carried out with quite a bit of creativity and genius. The fact that "there was a tool for that" regardless of what I was doing told me that there were some pretty creative people out there and that I wasn't the first one to face the challenge I was facing.

As a kid, I didn't really want to take the time to look for a specific tool. Who wants to do all that thinking and then all that searching? Sometimes, some of those more specific tools required a little more prep time, or they were not quite as handy as the everyday stuff. It seemed much more expedient to simply grab some more common tool at hand, like a wrench, a hammer, a screwdriver, or a saw, and force it to work. "Grab what's close to you and get going" was a mantra that I chanted and acted on far too many times.

Eventually, I found out that there's nothing like power tools. Those things can rip and tear and screw and unscrew faster than you can imagine. Certainly, electric tools were very good, but compressed air tools packed a punch you couldn't believe. When you hooked up the compressor, things were bound to be flying everywhere. Electric or compressed air, it really didn't matter. You use that kind of power, and you don't really need that specific tool, because that stuff will blow through the job one way or another. So who needs the right tool when you have 110 watts and 80 psi?

As you might imagine, when I didn't use the right tool, two things typically happened. Either I'd get the job done but not nearly as fast or clean or professional as it might have gotten done if I'd had the patience to get the right tool, or I'd completely blow the job and destroy a lot of things along the way, leaving me wondering what my aversion to getting the right tool was about in the first place. Typically, I ended up with a pathetically poor or pulverized job. The fact that "there's a tool for that" can be wonderful if you find it and use it, or it can be completely frustrating if you ignore it and blow through a job to the destruction of the job.

THE TOOL OF RECOGNIZING THERE'S A TOOL

In living out our lives, I think we need to recognize that whatever we come up against, "there's a tool for that." Sometimes we don't think there is any tool; there's no resource to deal with or engage the irritating obstacles or looming challenges that are facing us. At times, we face things we've never faced. When that happens, we can't come up with a tool because we don't even know enough of what we're facing to craft a tool for it. There's an underlying, albeit inaccurate assumption that if we haven't dealt with it before, neither has anyone else. So, we assume that our only recourse is to haphazardly grab the nearest tool and get to work.

Sadly, sometimes we're not astute enough to effectively discern the challenges around us and then carefully find the tool to deal with it. Rather, we often assume that no such tool exists, that the real challenge is to take what we have and have at it. We think that it's really all about being creative and innovative, of pulling together our assorted array of mismatched tools and figuring out how to apply them to some task for which none of them are really designed.

When we can't find a tool, we sometimes get flustered, riled, and insufferably peeved to the point that we throw up our hands, murmur some colorful language under our breath, and walk away from the situation altogether. In doing so, we end up leaving yet another piece of our lives lying broken when it need not be so.

THE TOOL OF CREATIVITY

Sometimes life is like that. Because it is, sometimes life demands the fullest exercise of our creativity. At times, circumstances will leave us with monumental challenges and only a handful of the most primitive tools to deal with them. We will all stand in places and have events transpire that are immeasurably bigger than the handful of sordid and banged up tools we have to deal with them. In these instances, the tool that we use is our creativity.

One of the greatest tools that we have is the ability to take our personal resources and use them in a manner that makes the sum total of them much greater than what any of them could achieve individually. Our creativity allows us to see not what our resources are, but what they could be if used in unique combination with each other. Creativity is the ability to expand on those tools that by themselves are limited by their own limited designs. It means seeing new possibilities in new combinations. Creativity means that nothing needs to be only what it is, but that things can be much more if they are used in a manner that's not quite as obvious as the obvious.

The Tool of Determination

Harriet Beecher Stowe wrote, "When you get into a tight place and everything goes against you, till it seems as though you could not hold on a minute longer, never give up then, for that is just the place and time that the tide will turn." Determination is not stubbornness, nor is it idealistic foolishness. It's not being naïve, stupid, or relentless in a manner that's nothing more than naïve and stupid. Rather, it is the belief that something is going to happen if we push it and press it far enough. Determination is a tool that causes us to drive our situation beyond what appears to be a conclusion, a failure, or a presumed dead-end. The tool of determination is exacted and exercised by understanding that stubbornness is simply bullheadedness for the sake of being bullheaded. Foolishness is proceeding without thought. Naiveté is ignorance as a choice. And being stupid is much more about intellectual laziness than it is about lack of intelligence. Determination is much more strategic than that. The tool of determination recognizes that persistence is not the exercise of futility but an understanding that additional pressure rightly exerted can move what seems to be immovable.

The Tool of Faith

Patrick Overton wrote that when pushed to the brink, "faith is knowing one of two things will happen: there will be something solid to stand on or you will be taught to fly." Faith is believing in something that you can't see and standing in the belief that something exists despite your inability to perceive it. With the whole concept of faith, we can rest in the knowledge that our challenges are not bound by limitations. We can engage our challenges with an eye set firmly on what we're facing while concurrently realizing that what we see is not all that there is. It recognizes that what we can't perceive is infinitely vaster than anything that we could ever possibly hope to perceive in a thousand life times, yet the daunting vastness of everything that we can't see is accessible to us, nonetheless. Faith, then, is a tool that dramatically expands the scope of what we can do and dramatically enlarges the possibilities.

THE TOOL OF WISDOM

Wisdom is often defined as the application of knowledge. Many people have knowledge, but they're not knowledgeable in the application of it. We can be book-smart, street-smart, and just plain smart. Yet, we can be stupid in the application of our smartness. Wisdom is the manner in which we carefully discern the challenges before us and then wisely draw from our knowledge base. Wisdom also freely recognizes that we may not have nearly enough information in the first place, and that at times we must put our efforts on hold and search out whatever information we need to make the right decisions. Wisdom demands that wisdom itself never be short-changed, abruptly utilized, or applied in some sort of arrogant manner. When we do that, we strip wisdom all the way down to bare-boned foolishness. Wisdom is a precious tool to be handled in keeping with its profound value.

SO MANY TOOLS

There are so many tools at our disposal. Sadly, we're often not introspective enough to discover the tools inherent within us, or we're too busy to care. Indeed, the tools are there. Somewhere inside of us, "there's a tool for that," or there's a tool to create a tool. We come with the ability to be equipped in a way that there will always "be a tool for that." If we can't find one within us or around us, God always has one that we can readily borrow. And so, you may want to take a tool inventory and see what's inside of you. You'll likely be quite surprised. As Dad said, "there's a tool for that."

CHAPTER 36

Killing the Sacred: Bludgeoning the Heart Out of Life

*"If anyone destroys God's temple, God will destroy that person; for God's temple is **sacred**, and you together are that temple" [emphasis mine].*

1 Corinthians 3:17

"A man is ethical only when life, as such, is sacred to him, that of plants and animals as that of his fellow men, and when he devotes himself helpfully to all life that is in need of help."

Albert Schweitzer

YOU'VE PROBABLY HEARD IT SAID before, "Nothing's sacred anymore." There seems to be a core truth in that statement that continually gathers a sad and rather disparaging kind of momentum. We attempt to domesticate the sacred as part of our reductionist efforts to suck the mystery right out of life and make it manageable. The era of rapid scientific advancement appears to embrace an underlying assumption that everything is quantifiable and therefore controllable. We feel that if we scrutinize it enough, we'll eventually make sense of it. Once we make sense of it, our knowledge of it places it within the realm of our control. We don't reverence that which we can understand and control. Where's the sacred in that?

It seems that we don't value much anymore in a sacred kind of way that makes something intensely worthy of our fullest admiration. There are very few things that capture our minds, not in the sense of curiosity, but in a striking kind of sense that leaves us nearly breathless and feeling miniscule by comparison. There is another kind of experience where we realize that we've suddenly crossed paths with something so far beyond the confines of our humanity that it defies explanation, and in effortless defiance, it begets reverence.

QUANTIFYING THE SACRED

Despite this kind of marvel, we seem to have embraced this slipshod and rather dubious view that our world is filled with things that we could randomly sort through and determine whether they have value or not. This "sorting" sometimes looks like a massive, blind, heathen horde rummaging through priceless treasures, belligerently shifting and sorting without a single thought for the precious artifacts they blithely and blindly toss aside. What is sacred is not recognized as sacred because we often won't grant it that place in our lives. We've ignored it long enough to forget what it looks like. And because we've completely forgotten what the sacred looks like, we don't know it well enough to even remotely recognize it when it brushes by us. Unfortunately, even if we could ascertain the sacred, our attitudes are such that we might not even care that it visited us.

DEFINITION OF THE SACRED

To talk about the sacred, I suppose that we need to have a fresh and somewhat re-energized understanding of it. The Merriam Webster Dictionary has several definitions for the word *sacred*. However, one definition paints in broad relief an essential and largely lost characteristic of the word that abruptly thrusts it off our bland canvases and makes it more than a colorless word or pathetically lifeless concept. That definition defines *sacred* as something "entitled to reverence and respect." That doesn't quite electrify the word with brilliant hues, does it? Neither do we find ourselves tingling because of such a definition. That might be because we've forgotten.

The definition suggests that there are things that have some inherent quality or qualities within them that are worthy of reverence and respect. Apparently, some things naturally possess characteristics that should elicit our utmost admiration. Larger life is not held hostage to the single, flat dimension that we aimlessly poke and plod around on a daily basis. There are things inexpressibly grander than we are that simply cannot be drawn down to the lowly place we occupy. There are things that won't be cracked by our intelligence or lassoed by scientific rigor. Life has things that evade the mind of man; man will always need to have something to pursue that he can't catch. Reverence is what we give those things that we can't catch.

Reverence assumes that these things are entitled to reverence and respect; otherwise, the definition of reverence itself makes no sense. Why we would define something that doesn't exist? Why would we suggest attributes that we can't apply to anything other than being a nice idea or an intriguing concept? A title without something real to adhere it to is just a dubious collection of uninhabited words. Therefore, there must be things in our world and probably in our own lives that are sacred and therefore revered.

WHAT THE SACRED ASKS OF US

We may avoid embracing the sacred or giving it due attention because of what it asks of us. The sacred asks many things of us that we often find too humbling to give. The sacred forces us to face the sometimes-terrifying limitations of our own tiny humanity. The sacred makes us embrace the distasteful fact that we are not little gods scampering about our worlds in god-like fashion, although we love to play the part and believe it to be so. The sacred resolutely returns the reality of our humanity to its proper place, and it restores the breathless expanse of everything that's beyond our humanity. Indeed, the sacred asks a lot of us. Therefore, we might consider the following:

THE SACRED ASKS US TO RECOGNIZE THAT WE CAN'T CREATE IT

It would seem that the truly sacred things in life are truly sacred not because we put those qualities within them, but because they have those qualities naturally. The sacred is sacred of its own accord and not because we took some sort of action to make it sacred. It would seem that if we can create it, it's probably not sacred because it doesn't reflect anything that's any more than who we are. *Sacred* implies something greater than us that in all probability didn't originate with us. Therefore, we can't create it, and we have to embrace it as superior to who we are and beyond what we can create of our own efforts.

THE SACRED ASKS OUR REVERENCE

So, what is the sacred? Too often, what's sacred to us is *us*. In essence, we reverence ourselves. Therefore, we grant ourselves unapologetic permission to define the sacred in whatever manner tickles our fancy. The sacred has a much better chance of getting some airtime in our lives if we are granted editorial license to take up the intellectual pen and define it a bit. Our desire to define it appears to be rooted in what it will do to us if we don't define it. If we don't define it, we automatically let it define itself, which could result in possible consequences for us. Therefore, we don't revere it. Rather, we define it, fooling ourselves in the defining that we've defined it into something mystically reverential. Actually, we've stripped it of reverence and respect and subjugated it to our thin whims and weak story lines.

THE SACRED ASKS THAT WE RELINQUISH CONTROL

If we can't control something we're probably not going to snuggle up to it and get cozy with it. If we can't control the course of a relationship or the steps to some goal, there's a good chance that we fear it because it could do us damage. If we control it, we're less likely to be hurt. So, we control out of fear. There's also the reality that if we can't control something, it may ask something of us that we're not willing to give, and if there's any give and take involved in it, we'd rather be on the receiving end of that deal. So, if there's any exchanging to be had, we can be on the plus side of the transaction by controlling that as well. The oddity is that if we control the sacred, it's no longer sacred. To embrace it, we must relinquish our desire to control it and our attempts to do so. Therefore, for many of us, this is a non-negotiable deal-breaker.

THE SACRED ASKS THAT WE PUT OURSELVES SECOND

The sacred requires submission—not a demanding, authoritative type of submission at all. Rather, the sacred requires a submission that's based on the reverence that we have for the sacred thing. It's a completely voluntary reverence wherein we place ourselves in subjection to that which is sacred. Truly sacred things can only be embraced voluntarily; forced submission is more akin to slavery. And slavery has no part in that which is truly sacred. However, if we're asked to serve the sacred or reverence it in some personally dethroning capacity, we often label it as demanding or brash, thrusting it into the same category into which we've crammed most of the rest of the world. If we don't elevate the sacred, it can no longer function as the sacred.

THE SACRED ASKS THAT WE LIVE A LIFE OF CONSTRAINT

The sacred naturally prompts a critical self-evaluation and a frank reconsideration of life. You can't brush up against the sacred, or have it brush by you, without it stirring some deep stuff. The sacred is that dynamically piercing light that penetrates into places and backlights areas that we either don't want exposed or didn't even know existed. The sacred is made up of that pure, non-compromising stuff whose essence is uncontaminated and uncompromised. So, when it we encounter it, it dramatically illuminates everything within us that's not pure or uncompromising. That experience can be troubling or transforming.

THE SACRED ASKS . . .

There's a marvelous aspect of life that we forfeit when we abandon the sacred. There exists a whole dimension of living that's elevated above and beyond us that we are privileged to touch, caress, and hold. Likewise, the sacred does the same with us. Rather, we choose to ignore it and throw out it. We lose irreplaceable gifts and phenomenal privileges when we lose the sacred. Our lives are flatter, the world's a bit darker, and we forgo the privilege of savoring some of the most precious essences that life has to offer. Embrace the sacred, invite it in, stand in awe of it, and let that action transform all of your other actions.

CHAPTER 37

Left Lane Living: Driving at the Speed of Life

"He replied, 'Because you have so little faith. Truly I tell you, if you have faith as small as a mustard seed, you can say to this mountain, "Move from here to there," and it will move. Nothing will be impossible for you.'"

—Matthew 17:20

"I saw a sign; it said left lane closed so I went someplace else."

—Jay London

LARRY ELDER SAID, "A GOAL without a plan is just a wish." How many of us have a bunch of wishes that are nothing but wishes and become nothing more than wishes? As time goes on, we get tired of wishing because our wishes come to nothing. We assume that wishes remain only that and are not capable of being moved from the vague and misty transparency of wishes to an actual reality. Wishes are just that—wishes, the hope of something more that will never be anything other than a hope. The "when you wish upon a star" mentality assumes that wishful hope is a magical sort of gesture, but it placates any tangible outcome to hopeful thinking. Therefore, we forgo the whole wonderful idea of dreaming and settle for the scrapes that life tosses at us.

THE RIGHT LANE OF LIFE

We end up in the traffic of life: the molasses-moving, pathetically congested, ever-frustrating right lane of traffic. The right lane of life is home to an endlessly illuminating sea of brake lights, the irritating jostling of stop-and-go traffic, and the distressing gridlock of everyone going nowhere while thinking that they're making progress. It's a slow motion parade that has nothing of the fun, energy, and celebration of a parade but has everything of celebration gone to rot in the right lane.

Once we're in the traffic of life, and we're firmly in the right lane, we set our speed to match the traffic around us. Whatever the life in front of us is doing, that's what we end up doing. Our cadence is determined by the bumper that we're following, and the one that's riding our bumper in the rear. We become a link in a long progression that settles into a methodical flow that devolves from going from one place to going nowhere. We end up doing nothing more than just maintaining some sort of general movement that eventually becomes all about the movement and has nothing whatsoever to do with a destination of any kind. In time, our destination is the right lane, and our goal is driving along with some sense of pride, progress, and commendable persistence.

ADOPTING THE DRIVE STYLES OF OTHERS

In the methodical doldrums and humdrum of the right lane, we eventually develop the driving styles of those around us. After awhile, we're moving along in a mediocre line of life's right lane, isolated and hemmed in less by the traffic itself and more by the routines that we've developed from being in the traffic. Sure, we're headed somewhere, but we're poking and plodding along as a small part of the traffic around us, not as people who are called to great destinations. We are a single link in a larger jam. The line of people who make up this traffic extends out beyond the horizon of our sight, leaving us with the sense that we just have to sit it out and let it work itself out. "Hang in there," we tell ourselves in some sort of hallowed hurrah. Bolstered by our own cheerleading, we do exactly that. How tragic.

Eventually, we forget our destination altogether because our entire focus is in keeping in pace with the traffic. We're paying so much attention to the stuff in the right lane that *all* we're doing is paying attention to the stuff in the right lane. Life becomes all about navigating the traffic—about watching the traffic and forgetting to ask why we're in the traffic at all. We quit asking what we're doing here, and we let the navigation of the traffic be our singular goal.

When that happens, it's indicative of the fact that we've forgotten our destination altogether. Our focus becomes driving down whatever road we're driving down, and our goal becomes navigating the road for the sake of navigating the road. In time, the right lane of life is all that we see and ultimately all that we know. Life becomes a one-lane road heading in one direction with one person in front of us and one person behind us. And our one goal is to stay on the road. The left lane is entirely forgotten, so much so that we have forgotten that it exists at all.

THE OTHER LANE

Life seems freer in the left lane of life. The left lane is the place where we go when the simple cadence and average speed becomes irritating or altogether intolerable. The left lane is where we have a greater sense of a larger goal and a lesser sense that life is about pacing ourselves based on everyone else. There's a responsible aggressiveness in the left lane—not a foolish type of aggression, but an aggression that's borne out of a refusal to bend to mediocrity and kneel to the status quo. There's a sense that life can open up when all that we see is congestion, whether that's the congestion that other people create in our lives or the congestion that we're so prone to create in our own heads.

The left lane is just a few scant feet over from the right lane, but it's miles apart in attitude. It's about refusing to ride the bumper in front of you or be ridden by the one behind you. The left lane is about breaking from what everyone else is doing and choosing to take a more active hand in where you're going and how you're getting there. It's about letting an open road give you room to map out your destination, rather than having that destination dictated by the taillight in front of you...that's dictated by the one in front of it. The left lane is for those who aren't afraid to press the accelerator a bit, pass a few pokey cars, and set their sights a whole lot farther down this road that we call life.

THE CONVICTION OF DESIRE

In her now classic bit of prose, Helen Keller wrote, "It is for us to pray not for tasks equal to our powers, but for powers equal to our tasks, to go forward with a great desire forever beating at the door of our hearts as we travel toward our distant goal." Left lane living is fueled by desire—passionate desire. It's a relentless, unforgiving desire that will constantly pound on the door of our hearts until we grant it the complete entrance into our hearts that it demands. It's a rightly obstinate, persistently ruthless, unashamedly robust sort of passion that will not permit the plodding cadence of right lane living. Desire demands what desire itself desires, and that is the expenditure of every drop of lifeblood in the life-giving pursuit of life itself. It's about the outright rejection of compromise. It's a casting off of the blood-sucking nature of fear and the agonizing tedium of worry. It's about the outlandish confrontation of any attitude, plan, destination, or emaciated goal that would do anything other than demand the fullness of our abilities and the totality of our allegiances. Its desire unleashed, which is life unfettered.

That kind of desire thrusts us into the left lane of our lives. With desire, we can't be any place else. The right lane of life becomes insufferable. Driving along with a weather eye on the plodding life in front of us and attention to the other plodding life behind us—as tightly reflected in our tiny rearview mirrors—becomes dreadful. In time, it will become completely unbearable, forcing us to seize the wheel and swerve out of the timid, double-lined right lane of our lives and roar into the momentum of the left lane.

THE POWER OF PASSION

If desire is what drives us to wrench ourselves out of the right lane and career into the left lane, passion is the accelerator. Alexander Pope wrote that "on life's vast ocean diversely we sail. Reasons the card, but *passion the gale*" (italics mine). Passion is the wind in our sails that blows in gale force. It's that unyielding and obstinate power that will not cease, despite how often we often keep the mainsails of our lives wrapped tight by the rigging of fear and the lanyards of practicality. Passion is the power that either drives, drags, or throws us forward with the momentum generated by its inexhaustible energy.

We can stay in the right lane and just let the left lane blow by us, wondering what in the world that was. We can see the left lane more as an annoyance that blows through the calm of our mediocrity, causing us some degree of consternation because it sometimes seems so intrusive and so uncomfortably fast. We can view the left lane as filled with a bunch of impatient people who let their arrogance dictate how hard they're pressing the pedal. Or, we can recognize it for what it is, let it fully fuel our lives and throw us forward in the left lane of life. We can bring all of the resources that we have together in order to harness the whole of it and be thrust forward toward horizon after horizon after horizon.

WHICH LANE?

One final thought that we haven't yet entertained. Sometimes, we're not in the right lane, nor are we in the left lane. Sometimes, we're not on the road at all. We've just chosen to wait it out, thinking that the road will lighten up at some point and present us with a more favorable journey. There are the rest-stop dwellers among us who've found some kind of solace in getting off the road altogether. For those of us who are these people, we'll probably never get on the road because it will never be as safe as we might like. So, we park and wait for nothing. And that is the most tragic journey I can think of.

So, which lane? Or, maybe we'll choose no lane at all and park it somewhere. The open road of life is exactly that: open. God has granted us endless highways to explore and numerous destinations in this thing called life. Indeed, it is an adventure designed by the Master Adventurer Himself. The left lane's calling, and it's open. So, which lane will it be?

CHAPTER 38

Lemmings and Sheep: The Role of Boundaries and Rules

"For such people are not serving our Lord Christ, but their own appetites. By smooth talk and flattery they deceive the minds of naive people."
—Romans 16:18

"There's a whiff of the lynch mob or the lemming migration about any overlarge concentration of like-thinking individuals, no matter how virtuous their cause."
—P. J. O'Rourke

WE FOLLOW. THAT'S WHAT WE seem to do the most. Whether that's following other people, organizations, a set of rules, a collection of standards, some belief system, the by-laws, the speed limit, a schedule, some game plan, or some set of ideas that we've laid out in our heads. We follow our "gut," we follow a map, and we follow the recipe. We follow at a distance, and we follow closely behind whatever we're following. We follow boldly and sometimes tentatively and with varying degrees of fear. Even at times when we think we're leading, we're often following because we're really doing nothing more than leading others in the larger process of following something or someone else.

Certainly, there are many times and numerous situations in life when following is completely appropriate and even necessary. Sometimes when we choose to follow, we're actually leading; the choice to follow is freely made in order to serve a purpose larger than ourselves. Often, following in a given situation is the best path to success—or even the path to eventual leadership. There are times and places to follow, but only times and places.

WELCOME TO THE HERD

Those times aside, we tend to be seekers of lines that we can fall into and follow. We're going through life trying to figure out where everybody else is going so that we get in the same pathetic line that they're already in. There's something social about lines. It's as if we're joining a larger effort and engaging in a unified manner with a host of like-minded people. Somehow, lines make us more than what we'd feel like standing alone. Somehow, lines suggest that we're committed to an effort larger than we are. We're part of the team. We're walking lockstep with an army of others. We're going to be part of a force that everyone else is going to have to reckon with. We're on the move, and because we are, things are going to change in this mass advance of humanity of which we're a part. The problem is it's probably not going in any particular direction other than the direction it happens to be wandering in before it goes in the next direction.

More likely, we tend to gravitate toward the herd because the only thinking that we need to do when we're following is how we maintain our place in line and not step on the heels of the guy in front of us. It's fairly simple and not very demanding at all. We have a natural tendency to follow because following tends to be the proverbial path of least resistance. We just go wherever everyone else is going. That sounds hopelessly pathetic, but if we examine our lives, in far too many cases, it's exactly what we're doing. We just grace what we're doing with a thin icing of independence and edge it with the frosting of determination so it doesn't look so much like herd stuff. Yet in essence, we're lemmings and sheep. Over time, the whole following thing devolves into a lifestyle that is lifeless.

WHAT FOLLOWING DOES TO OUR THINKING

In the whole process of following, what dictates where we go is the fact that everyone is going there too…wherever "there" is. Indeed, it's the herd mentality—since everybody is going somewhere in some seemingly united fashion, we assume "somewhere" must have been thought through enough to be deemed worthy of everyone going there. We think that following was a well thought out decision that had some sort of methodical cognitive processing behind it, intellectually convincing enough to compel everyone to head out in that direction.

In reality, that's often a thinly transparent assumption that leads us to believe that the rightness of choice or direction or belief is illustrated by how many people are doing it. Most often, the herd moves based on the movement of the herd. Rarely does it move on a general unifying consensus regarding some wisely and discreetly chosen destination. Most times, it's just wandering in a way that might pass for direction but isn't. That assumption is terribly dangerous, and it liberally propagates lemmings and sheep.

CRITICAL THINKING

Eventually, we lose the idea of critical thinking or the process of analysis. We don't consider why we're in the line we're in and if it's going where we really want to go. Dante Alighieri wrote, "Consider your origins: you were not made to live as brutes, but to follow virtue and knowledge." We don't live on instinct as brutes, responding to some primordial sense that drives what we do. Our lives aren't driven solely by a primitive fight for survival that results in primitive actions.

We're blessed with uncanny foresight and weighty intelligence to be proactive. We don't have to be slaves to the often mindless and blithering knee-jerk responses of being reactive. We've been granted the ability to access the resources of intellect, knowledge, wisdom, expertise, and discernment. We possess a vast bank of knowledge and a cavernous warehouse of life experience that is constantly receiving rich deposits as we move forward in our lives. We're able to amass massive amounts of information drawn from our own lives and to dramatically complement that information by learning from both the successes and failures of those who have walked alongside us and before us.

We can think. Thinking implies reasoning. It means that we go far beyond just accepting some perspective or philosophy simply because everyone else seems to be walking in lockstep with it. We have the ability to ask why everyone else is doing it and whether it has any real value. Reasoning means that we can adequately probe a situation and deftly tease out its innermost parts so that we can cleanly say "yes" to situations, other times say "no," and at yet other times perform a modification of sorts and come up with a competent decision that represents neither alternative but a blend of both. We're not sheep, and we're not lemmings. We're not a card-carrying member of the herd. We're not a part of the blind, entirely permissive mob that plods along because everyone else is plodding along. We are much more.

The Fear

Sometimes, the whole falling in line phenomena is less about our ability to analyze our choices and more about the fear of making choices. Sometimes, going against the grain elicits the consternation of some people, the piercing stares of others, and it can negatively light up the grapevine like no other. Often, people don't want to have their feathers ruffled, and we do that by stepping out of the herd.

In stepping out, we're making a statement that being a lemming or a sheep might not be being the best thing. Quite often, the inactions of others are exposed through our actions. If the herd is its own point of comparison, then it's going to look comparatively good because the herd is only held to its own standard, essentially because there is no other standard. That fact can make the pathetic look downright acceptable and even rather stellar.

Yet, when that one, single irritating person steps out of line and questions both the line and where it's going, the complacency of everyone else is illuminated in the light of that action. The reality that we're being complicit in some sort of group conspiracy is revealed. People who refuse to be lemmings and sheep suddenly throw out this alternate perspective that stands in stark contrast to the actions of everyone else. That contrast can be so revealing that it creates shame in the rest of the meandering lemmings and wandering sheep. That shame rarely causes those in the group to step back and ask what in the world they're doing and why they're doing it. Instead, it prompts a reaction to get the independent person back in line so that herd can once again rest in being nothing but the herd.

LEMMINGS AND SHEEP WE ARE NOT

We weren't made to wander in the mass of some meandering herd. We aren't lemmings, and we don't even come close to resembling sheep. Quite the opposite; we were designed for innovation, creativity, challenge, and solitary adventures on life's mountain peaks shared with other solitary souls who let the herd wander in valleys far below. Which will we be? Where and with whom will we walk? It's a question worth pondering every day.

CHAPTER 39

Magnificent Living: Taking Things for Granted

*"All this also comes from the LORD Almighty, whose plan is wonderful, whose wisdom is **magnificent"** [emphasis mine].*

—Isaiah 28:29

"Am I willing to give up what I have in order to be what I am not yet? Am I able to follow the spirit of love into the desert? It is a frightening and sacred moment. There is no return. One's life is charged forever. It is the fire that gives us our shape."

—Mary Richards

ALDOUS HUXLEY POINTEDLY POINTED OUT that "most human beings have an almost infinite capacity for taking things for granted." If you think about it, "infinite" is a rather extensive capacity, and we're quite adept at utilizing that capacity to its fullest extent. Taking things for granted means that they no longer garner our attention. They've lost their value to us. Because they've served us quite well and quite consistently, we develop the sense that they'll always be there, or that they're just supposed to be there. We assume that things occupy a place in our lives just because they're supposed to occupy a place. We often see things as an entitlement or an action we'd blithely ascribe to the norm. Our thinking comes to a screeching halt at the rather juvenile and careless idea that "things are just because things are." And so, we take things for granted.

IGNORED AND INVISIBLE

The incongruity of it all is simply that things that should demand our attention, or are at least deserving of it, are ignored. Gifts, talents, and personal abilities are exercised day in and day out but aren't seen in the exercising anymore. Relationships, material blessings, opportunities, assorted privileges, innumerable resources, and options beyond counting—they all become the norm, and the norm renders them visibly invisible. Because these things are not seen, they aren't cherished, since we are extremely quick to forget that which we've rendered invisible. People, resources, or abilities that should be held in high regard or seen as a privilege are categorized as the stuff of "stuff." What we can't see, we don't value because our slack attitude and slothful inattention have sentenced these precious things to the death-row realm of the invisible.

As we meander along and do this, things gradually fall unnoticed behind an invisible veil. That veil doesn't remove them. Rather, all of these things are smack-dab in front of us but are completely invisible to us. As they fall behind the veil of taking things for granted, their presence in our lives remains unchanged, yet because of their invisibility, their worth or value, which is often immense, is lost. We walk around with precious things, precious people, precious resources, precious talents, and precious opportunities that are completely invisible and therefore ignored.

Because we can't see it, we're on a mad hunt for some freshly miraculous stuff to replace what we can't see. We're a society perpetually starved for entertainment. We want to be played to and played for. What's the next bit of news and the latest sound bite and the trendiest trend? Where can I get my itch for excitement scratched? Because we're always looking for something new, that which is invisible is never found; after all, we're not looking for it. Not only are we not looking for it, we're not even anywhere close to where we left it. So we take astonishingly precious things for granted as they slip into invisibility, and we leave them behind in our sweaty and fevered search for something new.

Through inattention and the amassing of a pile of stuff, we take things for granted. That fundamentally means that precious things have fallen off our radar under the pretense that they're just supposed to be. Because they become invisible, we amass more stuff to fill the void we think is left. In time, that stuff falls to the same dreaded death-row cell of invisibility. The whole mentality of "it just is" is a certain death sentence for thankfulness. It's the brutal execution of a sense of privilege. It senselessly murders a sense of the magnificent, and it mindlessly crucifies every blessing that God would liberally and lovingly pour into our lives. When these things die, a massive part of our lives die right along with them.

MAKING THE INVISIBLE STRIKINGLY VISIBLE

We don't often think of actions that show us as rich, that seize the strength and wonder of our inherent humanity and cause us to do great things. We miss the fact that sometimes just getting through a typical day requires feats of strength, tenacity, courage, and outright determination. Most often, life's about survival and getting ahead, if we can even pull these off. But we tend not to think that the commonplace and mundane are quite often feats of great wonder, drawing from deep within us prodigious abilities that we've taken for granted.

We never stop and think that the sun is always rising and setting all at the same time, all the time. It never crosses our minds that a single average mature tree can have as many as a two hundred and fifty thousand leaves on it. We've never even thought about the fact that a single bee will pollinate one thousand six hundred blossoms a day for forty-five days until it dies. We look at a lawn and never realize that there are approximately one hundred and eight million, nine hundred thousand blades of grass per acre. That's some astonishing stuff that's all in plain sight yet entirely invisible to us.

Bill Moyers wrote, "Creativity is piercing the mundane to find the marvelous." Is it possible that the mundane is really the marvelous in quiet disguise, and that creativity is figuring that out? Is it possible that in their own way, all things are marvelous with a type of marvel that's marvelously unique to them? Could it be possible that everything is marvelous in its own way, and that life is nothing but marvelous things on top of other marvelous things as they sit right next to a thousand other marvelous things? And is it possible that each one of us is marvelous in just the same way?

Have you ever considered the possibility that great feats may really be nothing more than an intentional and focused use of the resources that exist within the person—marvelous resources that we have an ample and similar supply of ourselves? Have we allowed the marvelous within us to be taken for granted so that its dollar value has been degraded to pennies when in reality it's all priceless beyond any collection of pennies, regardless how massive? And are we in a place where we need to consider all of this because we've underpriced and marginalized our worth through the persistent effort of taking things for granted?

Taking Things for Granted by Mental Laziness

So we're robbed, and we're the culprits who did it. We've used the highly effective tool of taking things for granted. Part of our taking things for granted involves our dogged mental and emotional laziness. Things of true worth in life don't clamor for our attention. They don't attempt to seize the stage of our lives in some brazen display, touting their worth as they strut back and forth. Things of great value don't gravitate toward the limelight or top billing.

Rather, the things of true worth are to be sought out, looked for, and discovered in a passionate search for the stuff of life. It's a rejection of all the plastic and veneers, all the things that attempt to replicate the real stuff. It takes effort to find the things of real value— great and unrelenting effort that we often don't want to exert. Plastic and veneers are much, much easier, so we've got loads of them. We take for granted "taking things for granted."

TAKING THINGS FOR GRANTED BY ENTITLEMENT

And then there's the whole "I'm owed" mentality. Things are, just because they're supposed to be. This whole deal we call life is obviously supposed to come with all the finery and accessories. It's just part of the package. It's just supposed to be. So why value a possession or person when it's not a gift, treat, surprise, bonus, or nice addition that somebody thought would tickle our fancy? The package that extra stuff comes in is a bit of icing on the cake of entitlement, but it's not the cake. The cake is just supposed to be, and so it is. Entitlement is toxic, tragically transforming blessings to bare-bones stuff and priceless gifts to accessories that are ours solely by virtue of our birth. We take for granted "taking things for granted."

TAKING THINGS FOR GRANTED BY PERMISSION

It's quite amazing how many things we can give ourselves permission to do. Sometimes, we give ourselves permission to tolerate what we shouldn't, which is likely the worst kind of permission to grant ourselves. Tolerating something implies that we probably shouldn't be doing it in the first place, but we've chosen to do it anyway. There's a dash of ignorance and a pound or two of stupidity in a lot of the permission that we grant ourselves. There's a turning away, a bit of ethical "sleight of hand" and some mental "nip and tuck" that numbs us enough so that we can pass on our integrity without really feeling that we've passed. So we give ourselves permission to take many things for granted. We repeat this to the point that we take for granted "taking things for granted."

TAKING THINGS FOR GRANTED BECAUSE IT'S THE NORM

Sometimes we look around and try to find people doing the things that we've questioned doing. Somehow, if someone else is doing the stuff we find questionable, their actions lend whatever they're doing just enough legitimacy for us to do it. If someone else is doing it, we sometimes feel that we can step over the line just enough to dabble in the behavior and then jump back to the other side of that line. So, in a world that sloughs things off, we do the same. We take for granted what those around us take for granted. They reinforce our actions, and we reinforce theirs. In time, we don't even realize what we're doing, and we take for granted "taking things entirely for granted."

BREAKING THE HABIT

Magnificent living involves not taking the magnificent for granted. It's a refusal to marginalize the wonder of life by placing it behind some veil, invisible and lost. It's refusing to engage the sloth of mental laziness, the selfishness of entitlement, the egotism of permission, or the mediocrity of the norm. It's refusing all the tricks that would suppress the miraculous and being willing to live swallowed in the wonder of the world around us and within us. Live in wonder and it lives around you.

CHAPTER 40

Mining Memories: The Tool of Memories

*"Tell them that the flow of the Jordan was cut off before the ark of the covenant of the LORD. When it crossed the Jordan, the waters of the Jordan were cut off. These stones are to be a **memorial** to the people of Israel forever" [emphasis mine].*

—Joshua 4:7

"[Memory is] a man's real possession . . . In nothing else is he rich, in nothing else is he poor."

—Alexander Smith

SO, WHAT'S UP WITH MEMORIES? We all have hoards of them, apparently endless reams of them that run a seemingly impossible gamut of times, places, and people. Our memories encompass a boundless array of events. They store everything from life's most exquisite vistas captured by our eyes, to deeply surging emotions netted by the heart, to the slightest sounds and wispiest scents that wafted by both ear and nose. We remember what things felt like to the touch and what it was like to be touched. We can recall the delicately rich flavor of cold vanilla ice cream on listless summer nights and the frothy warmth of thick hot chocolate on biting winter evenings. We can reach back across the obscure horizons of the decades and recall a favorite tricycle, a cherished pet, or something as simple as a Grandma's loving hug.

Memories allow us to recall relationships lost, but likewise retrieve the fathoms deep undercurrent of emotions that ran along with them. They permit us ready access to loved ones long gone so that what remains is far more than an untended grave and weathered headstone. They allow us to ascend towering trees and propel ourselves skyward on the playground swings of our childhood. They can likewise haunt us with memories of dark times and painful moments. They are a living, breathing, pulsating porthole that allows us to live fully in the present with a vivid connection to the past. They then allow us the privilege to live within the full breadth of our entire existence.

Memories can be crystal clear and clean in their recollections. They can likewise be fuzzy, misty-like, and somewhat fluid, creating dramatic and moving renderings of our past from the abstract, to the surreal, to something quite conventional. Memories preserve what would otherwise be lost; they create a means by which to redeem ourselves through the lessons learned and adjustments made because we can recall it all enough to effectively learn from it.

WHAT ARE MEMORIES?

Are memories just sights and sounds and moments and experiences filed somewhere in some methodical filing cabinet located in the gray fissures of our brains? Are memories about some internal hard drive that collects all this stuff for retrieval at some critical or possibly opportune moment? Clearly, memories have a vitally important place in our lives; otherwise, why would we have them in such wonderful and woeful abundance? The ability that we have to store and recall information and experiences and feelings serves a multitude of indispensible purposes. In fact, it's likely that we simply couldn't live without the mind's ability to remember and to recall. If we could, we would certainly be so much the poorer.

Memories and the ability to recall things would appear to be incredibly, possibly indescribably important. The question is this: do we maximize this ability? Do we utilize this marvelous faculty as fully and as completely as we could or should? Have we ever even considered the magnitude of this seemingly fathomless resource, or do we embrace it as little more than a tool to reminisce or a curse that causes us to remember that which we'd much prefer to forget? Does memory become just the stuff of curious trivia or abundant fodder for colorful conversation? Or is it possible that this ability is far more valuable and more indescribably powerful than we even begin to realize?

It's possible that we don't even come close to understanding what this amazing resource can do. We coddle it, and we curse it. We sheepishly peer into it; at other times, we leap face-first into it. Sometimes we reach a frightened finger out to tap it in order to see if it's safe, and at other times we run away from it as far and as fast as our legs will carry us. Regardless of what we do with it, have we forfeited a phenomenal resource? Because we do, we leave it languishing as some sort of all too common process that readily generates trivia and information but lacks life-altering substance.

MEMORY FEEDS US

Amy Tan wrote, "Memory feeds imagination." Memory is the vast storehouse that feeds the richest parts of our deepest selves from its inventory. It's the rich and prolific foodstuff from which the marvel of our core humanity is luxuriantly nurtured. Memory refuses to grant us permission to live solely in the one-dimensional realm of the present. Instead, it affords us the opportunity to live in the flourish of the present while simultaneously sipping fully on the many variant flavors of the past. Memory can seamlessly draw from both the past and the present, more than sufficiently feeding our creativity so that we can live with flourish in the present and robustly create an innovative future.

MEMORY PRESERVES

Memory is that thing that will not allow life to listlessly pass by and be forever lost in the passing-by. Life comes by once, and if it were not somehow captured in the passing, we would hold it only for the moment that we have it, and then it would be forever gone. We would be creatures of the moment only, and we would be unable to take every moment and use those moments to build on every other moment. Memory allows for the amassing of a prolific array of building blocks rather than living with the flatness of holding onto the building block of the moment and having to forfeit it for the building block of the next moment and then the moment after that. Memory preserves in order to build.

MEMORY MAXIMIZES THE STOREHOUSE OF THE MIND

The human mind is incomprehensibly vast. Such is the extent of the mind that we're not even remotely capable of understanding what it can do. The only limitation that the mind has is the amount of information and experiences that we choose to put into it, not the capacity to store it. If we leave the mind empty, if we're unable to seize each moment and store those moments in the mind's vast storehouse for retrieval, the immense size of our minds simply wouldn't matter. Why foolishly squander the cavernous resource of the mind by leaving its vast enclaves empty and barren? Why would we let empty space define us?

MEMORIES BUILD ON THEMSELVES

Tyron Edwards wrote, "Contemplation is to knowledge what digestion is to food—the way to get life out of it." If we simply see memories as memories, as nice or not-so-nice places to walk around and reminisce about, we won't mine the riches in them in order to enhance their riches. We walk through our memories for many reasons, but typically not to submerge ourselves in them in order to let them build upon themselves. Typically, our trip into them is similar to a casual jaunt and more superficial than serious; it can be likened to a stroll rather than an expedition, or a walk in the park versus parking ourselves in the park. We miss the fact that memories build upon themselves in a prolific flowering that makes the sum total of the memories greater than their individual parts. Memories expand in their encounters with other memories.

MEMORIES MARK HISTORY

Memories are the files that hold our histories. Histories grant us an undeniable and powerfully sustaining sense of purpose as they recite our paths. In reciting our paths, we develop a sense that our lives were not woven from the fabric of randomness but follow a rational progression that suggests meaning and intent. Memories map out a path taken that permits us to see a rhyme and reason to what appeared to be randomness. They allow us to see our lives in retrospect and, in doing so, to identify footprints that, from the distance afforded by memory, are anything but wandering. It's here that we come to understand that our apparently meaningless and misdirected lives have a whole lot more purpose to them than we'd ever imagined. In such a telling discovery, we can see that our lives had a rationale that suggests undeniable purpose. Undeniable purpose leads to undeniable greatness.

REMEMBERING MEMORIES

You might be well advised to wade into the vast seas of your memories. Memory is too often potential untapped, identity forsaken, history rejected, and growth dodged. All too often, they are riches never cashed in, storehouses padlocked, and unimaginable opportunities starved and gone begging. We don't wade into our sea of memories; more often than not, we don't even go to the beach. Yet, memory is a rich storehouse to which only we have privileged access. It is ours alone to draw from. Such a journey is potentially rich—certainly richer than meandering or running. Don't live in your memories, but visit them often. Don't set up shop in your past, but liberally draw off its wealth. It will exponentially expand your life.

CHAPTER 41

Traditions:
A Sorely Needed
Grounding

"Jeremiah composed laments for Josiah, and to this day all the male and female singers commemorate Josiah in the laments. **These became a tradition** *in Israel and are written in the Laments" [emphasis mine]."*

—2 Chronicles 35:25

"At the beginning of the nineteenth century we abandoned tradition; it's at that point that I intend to renew it because the present is built on the past just as the past was built on the times that went before it."

—Adolf Loos

WE LIVE IN A CULTURE that's on a seemingly crazed mission to embrace whatever the newest thing is. We're diligent about looking out for everything from the latest fad, to the most current style, to the latest political agenda, to the newest thing that generates the biggest hype in the freshest way. We want to know about the newest book or computer game or cell phone application or travel destination or lingo. We want to know the latest philosophy about the latest philosophy. We want to know all of the trends, as well as the trends of all of the trends. We're all over what's in and what's out. We want to know who's dating who and who's through with who. If there's a new gadget or gizmo that's out, we don't necessarily want to know if it works, but we do want to know if it's becoming trendy or in vogue. What color is in this season? What's on the New York Times best-seller list; are people tending toward granite or tile; what's the newest investment scheme; and are people going with more of a shag look or Berber carpeting?

What's additionally interesting is that we spend tons of time watching what's coming in and what's going out so that whenever something finally gets here or gets gone, we're already ahead of it. We've determined that it's simply not enough just to keep up with the trends. We have this thing about staying trendy to the point that we need to predict the trends in order to be ahead of the trends. The airwaves are full of this stuff, keeping us up-to-date about being up-to-date so that we're not caught not being up-to-date. It's running forward at a million miles an hour and in doing so ripping up, tearing out, and throwing away everything that's not part of whatever it is that's come or is coming.

The Past as Irrelevant

It's odd, but with this kind of radical fast-forward mentality, the past is only good to the degree that it helped us get to the present and assists us in getting to the next place. The past is like a step on a really long staircase that we're only using to go up, with no intention of ever coming down. Because that's the case, the last step has value in that it got us to the step that we're on now. However, once the previous step has served its purpose in getting us to the place we are now, it's irrelevant and so it's discarded. The past has no lasting value, so it's forsaken, irreverently cast aside, blithely abandoned, and summarily forgotten.

With this pithy mentality, the present is presumed as being enough. We don't need to live in the past or ponder it; in fact, we often view that as a worthless expenditure of energy. We certainly shouldn't carry any of it into the present. In truth, the past is often viewed as burdensome, cumbersome, and unnecessary baggage, and bereft of anything of value. Its worth and whatever resource that it possessed was completely used up in getting us here, so why carry it if there's nothing left of it? It becomes an unnecessary liability, being carted around like dead weight, and being nothing more than a hindrance to everything that lies ahead. It can be a confining rubric that doesn't give the present ample space to breath or the future enough real estate to expand freely. And so, we dump it, recklessly casting it aside in favor of something new, fresh, and better.

THE FUTURE AS IMPOSSIBLE WITHOUT THE PAST

Yet, is the future possible without the past? The future is constructed upon the building blocks of the past. To assume that the future is entirely fresh and new is to miss the fact that the future is simply the past being replayed in different ways, unique ways, and possibly more creative ways. The future is human beings playing out their desires, their fantasies, their hopes, their dreams, their aspirations, their self-centered agendas, and their selfish appetites in the same way that they've played them out throughout the span of history. It just has a little bit of a different face on it given the advances in technology, the leaps in science, various social advances or reversals and the like, but it's the same. The future is the past wearing different clothing. As a wise man said in Ecclesiastes, "There is nothing new under the sun."

The future is not life minus the past. The future is the past refined, sharpened, and tempered. The past is not just the way that we got here. The past holds the key elements from which the present is shaped and the future is cast. It's not something to run from or discard out of the assumption that it's old, outdated, and antiquated. The past is nothing less than foodstuffs stored for future consumption, an immense storehouse from which the raw material of the future is compiled and constructed. Take away the past, and the present immediately vanishes, leaving the future a complete impossibility.

Jack Kerouac wrote that "great things are not accomplished by those who yield to trends and fads and popular opinion." If we are based solely in the lessons and realities of the present, we live in a singularly single dimension. We focus on nothing more than the present, which is a terribly thin slice of time. The overwhelming majority of existence isn't lived in the present. Existence itself is massively expansive, cascading in torrents from an eternal past and plummeting over the falls of an eternal future. We are only able to dip our fingers briefly in but one minutely small place in this massive torrent of time; we call that place the present. The "now" is a whisper-thin slice of the entirety of existence.

With that being the case, it would appear logical that most of life isn't lived in the now. The vast array of experiences, events, lessons, accomplishments, advances, gains, losses, storehouses of wisdom, and warehouses of knowledge are somewhere else. Indeed, they reside in what transpired before the "now." Trends, fads, and popular opinion are most often the jilted stepchildren of the present and estranged family members of the rich and deep family of the past. When we yield to them, we yield to their shallowness and their fragility. We yield to a single dimension of living.

TRADITIONS

Susan Lieberman landed on the idea of traditions when she wrote that "family traditions counter alienation and confusion. They help us define who we are; they provide sturdy benchmarks that are steady, reliable and safe in a confusing world." Traditions are a grounding that we don't have to create in order to be grounded. They are the compilation of lives lived before us and the experiences that transpired. The lessons learned, the losses experienced, and the things that are worthy of investment as well as those that are not worthy of anything are packed into the ornate package of traditions. Traditions are wondrously fashioned from the falls and pitfalls, the wealth of glorious advances, and the humiliating lessons of retreats. The gleaning of the golden threads of life amid soiled fabric of time, and the sweet nectars excruciatingly extracted from experiences both sweet and less than sweet are all packaged in traditions.

The wonder of traditions is that these priceless treasures are handed to us by others who obtained them. They are a gift, handed to us in the package of tradition without our having to have sacrificed to mine and refine them. Traditions hold within them generations of experience and wealth that this thin slice of time within which we live could never and will never be able to replicate. Traditions are expansive, importing into our lives the lives of those who lived before us. They permit us to experience a part of their journey, a piece of their hearts, a handful of their lessons, and a heart full of their emotions. Traditions make life three-dimensional, allowing us to live both now and then—an opportunity that coalesces into a life expansive beyond a life that might live in just one or the other.

Traditions provide that guiding function where the advances of the present are steered by the steady hand of the past. They ground us when constant innovation is always changing the ground beneath our feet. Traditions bind us to each other, throwing across the chasms of our individual lives steel cables that allow us to cross over to one another in the communion of one human being with another. They give us a common heritage, a point of steady reference in a world that's always rising and falling on the tides of change. They enrich, enliven, and recharge. They are priceless. They are unquestionably essential to living life with a fullness that's beyond ourselves and our time.

Finally, traditions give us permission to add to them in the marvelous advance of time. We are permitted the privilege of adding the scent our own lives to the larger scent of endless other aromas that make up the perfume of traditions. We can add a facet that expands all the other facets. We can bring some unique aspect that ties all the other aspects together in a manner that emboldens and enriches the tradition. We can add parts of ourselves that will be enfolded into the various traditions and passed to generations to follow, some of which we know and some of which are yet to be born.

Traditions are far more than dreary theatrical performances and stuffy rituals. They are not antiquated relics held over from a bygone era. They are not heirlooms encased in glass or preserved in the folds of a tattered family Bible. They embody lessons and precious mementos learned by generations of people who packaged those lessons and mementos in the form of traditions so that they might be transmitted down the corridor of time. Traditions are the efforts of others to keep the wealth of the past from dying in the annals of the past. You may wish to re-evaluate, reclaim, and restore traditions to your life. It will revolutionize your life.

CHAPTER 42

"Now I Lay Me Down to Sleep": Mom and Dad's Bedtime Prayer

*"One day Jesus was praying in a certain place. When he finished, one of his disciples said to him, 'Lord, **teach us to pray**, just as John taught his disciples'" [emphasis mine].*

—Luke 11:1

"More things are wrought by prayer than this world dreams of."
—Alfred, Lord Tennyson

IT WENT SOMETHING LIKE THIS: "Now I lay me down to sleep, I pray the Lord my soul to keep. If I should die before I wake, I pray the Lord my soul to take. God bless Mommy, Daddy, Mark, Brett, and Granny. Amen." Simple.

I recited that prayer thousands of times as kid. It comes to my memory today as clearly as it did those many years ago. It's wonderfully simple and joyously profound. Its words shaped and softly molded my tender soul as an infant and then as a child. It drew a soft blanket of warmth over my bed every night, and it calmed my heart when life turned dark. That simple prayer became a marvelous conduit of connection, creating a place each night where I could connect with God in days that sometimes seemed completely full of Him and in other days that seemed entirely void of Him. Its words were an anchor of iron proportions, dropped into seas churning and calm, tumultuous and restful. Their simplicity held me fast, and their depth held me strong. I am warmed when I recite them even today. At times, I have found myself as an adult reciting their simple words in the middle of my most complex times. There is something timeless about them.

PRAYING AS STIMULATING INTIMACY WITH PEOPLE

But they were never prayed alone. On the edge of my twin bed sat Mom, Dad, or sometimes both of them. The words of this simple prayer were recited in unison, creating a corporate simplicity that lent even greater power to them. There's an intricate weaving of souls that's incalculably rich when others join us in engaging the infinite. Joining another in prayer accelerates our humanity to peaks and points that we don't even understand. We can walk through the everyday challenges with people and find a rich and ever-developing camaraderie in the journey. But when we seize the soul and thrust it heavenward in prayer, and when we do that in the company of others who are doing the same thing, there is a unity that exceeds any other activity man can describe.

All I know is that such an activity is powerful; it exceeds words to encapsulate it, and it sets us in places that we're supposed to live in but rarely visit. When we pray with others, our tiny walls collapse to reveal endless vistas that dwarf our fears and give our pain perspective. Praying together takes our limitations and allows us to see that our limitations are nothing more than our fears in disguise. "Now I lay me down to sleep," prayed with Mom and Dad, ushered me into heavenly places and introduced me to vast spaces far beyond my simple bedroom and far beyond my life.

THE ACID TEST

Samuel Chadwick said that "prayer is the acid test of devotion." It is the indication of how devoted we are to God. Over any and all things, it is the gauge of our love for Him and our commitment to Him. That's so because it's the daily enterprise of putting all of our interests, all of our desires, all of our agendas, all of our goals, all of the things that incessantly clamor for our attention, and all other loves behind us in order to focus exclusively and selflessly upon God. Prayer is risking that time spent with God is not time spent away from other pressing needs. It's saying that time spent with God is allowing God to spend time with our pressing needs while we're spending time with Him. It's the exercise of our priorities rather than stewing in the contemplation of our priorities. Prayer is an intentional action of the abandonment of self in favor of the focus and worship of God. That is the acid test.

But the acid test of our relationship with others is partnering with them in prayer. It's joining others in prayer as a means of bringing them before God, and them only. It's not about us or any thin shade of us. Our needs and our agendas are rendered entirely invisible and wholly absent, wiped off the slate of prayer. It's where we relinquish our agendas, completely write off any potential gains, and stand solely in the stead of another. Prayer is about partnering with others and bringing their needs before God without a shred of consideration for ourselves. It's making ourselves invisible so that another is rendered more visible than a single soul can be alone. It's pristine selflessness.

The acid test is setting the self aside and praying not to bring one's own needs before God, or to bring oneself before God, or to seek some blessing large or small. It's not about slick secondary agendas or thinking how good we look praying for other people. Martin Luther wrote, "Our prayer must not be self-centered. It must arise not only because we feel our own need as a burden we must lay upon God, but also because we are so bound up in love for our fellow men that we feel their need as acutely as our own." Genuine prayer is about bringing someone else and his or her needs before God with nothing of ourselves clouding, polluting, or contaminating that action. It's keeping oneself entirely out of the equation in every way, shape and form. It's perfecting invisibility out of our perfect love for another. That kind of prayer is humanity made divine.

In commenting on the state of prayer today, Evan Roberts wrote, "Prayer is buried, and lost, and Heaven weeps." However, when we partner in this manner with others, prayer is living in a way that nothing else lives. It is anything but lost. Instead, it guides us when we are lost. And when we pray like that, heaven does not weep. Instead, it shouts with a commanding joy that thunders down its corridors and reverberates out into the infinite stretches of the cosmos itself. Selfless prayer on the behalf of others upends mountains, transforms the landscape, infuses life despite how barren the deserts might be, obliterates obstacles, and brings light to places where light is unknown. Selfless prayer topples towering obstructions, expunges darkness, expels fear, and exorcises things we thought to be immovable. Prayer in partnership is corporate humanity doing the phenomenal.

MOM AND DAD'S PRAYERS

"Now I lay me down to sleep." That's what that simple prayer uttered every night with Mom and Dad did for me. These two adults set their lives entirely aside, sat on the bedside of a heavy-eyed child, and spoke those words into his life. They put their own scars aside. They forfeited their own struggles and ignored the uncertainty that often dogged their steps and haunted their days. They pressed past financial fears, the exhaustion that depleted their own hearts, the issues that lay scattered throughout their extended families, and they bowed over me in prayer.

They held the hand of this tired child and prayed everything for him and nothing for themselves. They faced adversity that I couldn't comprehend until I faced them in my own life as a frequently weary adult. They scaled mountainous obstacles that I had no idea existed for them. They often peered into uncertain futures and prepared to put themselves to bed only to face challenges the next day. Yet, in that simple bedroom, their prayer was only for me. I am amazed and humbled by what they did each night, stooped over the tired child that I was.

PRAYER IN A WORLD OF SELFISHNESS

The first question is "are we going to pray?" Anything we think about prayer is entirely meaningless unless we pray. We can think about prayer, dissect it, read about it, theologize it raw, create creative structures to do it, take polls as to its effectiveness, work to squeeze it into our calendars, and contemplate it from a million different angles. We can do a whole lot of thinking that's often followed by a whole lot of nothing. But it's doing it that unleashes its power. No power comes from the study of it, but great power comes from the execution of it.

The second question is "who are we praying for?" The question might be better framed, "what's our agenda for prayer?" We are commanded to pray for ourselves, and that is both good and fitting. But if prayer ends there, it never really began. It calls for sitting on the bedside of a world that's hurting and lost, taking it by the hand and praying for it, clear of our own agendas.

That world comes in the form of people: spouses, children, neighbors, coworkers, and people we pass by. It has the face of organizations, governments, societal issues, and societal woes. It has the voice of crying children, weeping adults, destitute families, and tearful marriages. It has the eyes of the blind as well as those who prefer blindness to that which they see in their lives. A world in need of selfless prayer is all around us. Will you pray? Will you pray with no attention toward self? Will you engage in a rigorous discipline that that will change you and your world? "Now I lay me down to sleep." Pray it!

Conclusion

SOMEHOW ALONG THE WAY, WE seem to have lost
the simple truths. It seems that they've become cumbersome or irrelevant, or they get in the way of our agendas. We've labeled them
as outmoded, outdated, or simply out of touch. We take license with
our independence and manufacture truths of our own making, or
we simply make up truths as we go along. In creating and recreating our existence, we likewise create and recreate the truths of that
existence.

I can think of few things more damaging than creating our own
truths. Indeed, it is hard to imagine anything more diminishing to
the fullest living out of our lives than coming up with our own
truths about our lives. It's terribly difficult to visualize anything that
will destroy an individual or a nation any quicker and with greater
efficiency than building our own truths as a means of indulging our
own desires.

UNWELCOME ASSUMPTIONS

This line of thinking would presume the preexistence of truth, that
truth completely predates and entirely supersedes man. It presumes
that there are foundational and immovable truths in existence that
wholly circumvent man and to which we are subject, whether we
like that or not. It assumes that we are not necessarily masters of
our own fates and that we are accountable to something larger than
we are.

This kind of thinking would also presume that there is something called "truth" in the first place. It would suggest the presence of absolutes and that life is not conditional upon our whims and our fancies. It means that certain things can't and won't be tinkered with and that truth is one of those things. It would steadfastly hold to the idea that discovering these truths is infinitely more valuable and phenomenally more enriching than engaging in any futile attempt to change truth or create new truths. These are two rather forthright assumptions that frequently find great opposition in our world today.

THE PURPOSE OF THIS BOOK

This book has been about steadfastly believing in these kinds of truths and revisiting them in order to give people like you and me flecks of truth to tackle mountains of adversity. The premise that consistently undergirded this entire book is that simple truths are simply real and simply powerful. At the core of every challenge, there are simple truths that make up the foundation and fabric of that challenge, and that because that's the case, simple truths are the key to engaging, combating, dismantling, and destroying the challenges.

This book has been about rediscovering the simple truths by providing a fresh, clean, and practical look at simple truths. Yet, it's much more than simply revisiting and reacquainting ourselves with these truths by a simple reading and entertaining pondering. Rather, it's about the aggressive implementation of them in every arena of our lives. We read them, ponder them, find ourselves inspired by them, and become reinvigorated by our visit with them. But unless we apply them, they are much like a book on a shelf: full of information never applied.

It's my hope that this book will become a point of continual reference for you. May you repeatedly refer to these truths, drawing from them and allowing them to breathe something fresh and hope-filled into your circumstances. May they likewise invigorate you, inspire you, lift you, and fill your life with the nectar of vibrant and life-giving truth. In short, may they be utterly transforming. As

He has a way of doing, Jesus himself put it best when he said, "Then you will know the truth, and the truth *will set you free*" (John 8:32) [emphasis mine]. It's my deepest hope that the truths shared in this book have done and will continue to do exactly that for you. Truly, may you be blessed.

Readers may also be interested in other books by
CRAIG D. LOUNSBROUGH

AN AUTUMN'S JOURNEY:
Deep Growth in the Grief and
Loss of Life's Seasons

Genres: Christian Living, Grief
Paperback: 160 pages
ISBN: 9781935507581

We live in a culture that is desperate to avoid loss. We chose to fight it because we assume that it has come only to unfairly steal and inflict terrible pain. Loss is seen as the rogue enemy and heartless foe, rather than an opportunity for immense and improbable growth. It's in loss that some of the richest and rarest of life's lessons lay buried, eagerly waiting to be deeply mined and unearthed. In the deepest pain God does the deepest work. *An Autumn's Journey: Deep Growth in the Grief and Loss of Life's Seasons* does not loosely gloss over loss or provide shallow prescriptions and weak formulas for our grieving. Rather, it aggressively embraces both grief and loss, bringing fresh eyes to these times in our lives in order to draw out of them the marvelous riches that we all too often miss.

Also by
CRAIG D. LOUNSBROUGH

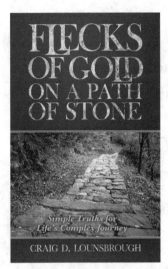

FLECKS OF GOLD ON A PATH OF STONE:
Simple Truths for Life's Complex Journey

Paperback: 240 pages
ISBN: 9781935507888

We live in a terribly complex world. Yet simple truths are what life is constructed upon. Sadly, these simple truths are often lost in the complexity of life or are deemed grossly inadequate in dealing with life's seemingly insurmountable challenges. The reality is that simple truths make for remarkably profound changes. They remove massive obstacles and provide stunning clarity to life's trials. They richly inspire us and deeply ground us in something that's core to who we are—something entirely unchangeable and unshakeable. This book contains those simple truths richly explained, practically expanded upon, and relevantly integrated into life's realities in a manner that brings fresh insight, rejuvenated hope, and desperately needed resources to all of us who struggle through the complexities of life.

For more information about
Craig D. Lounsbrough
&

FLECKS OF GOLD ON A PATH OF STONE
please visit:

www.craiglpc.com

....

For more information about
AMBASSADOR INTERNATIONAL
please visit:

www.ambassador-international.com
@AmbassadorIntl
www.facebook.com/AmbassadorIntl